AIRCAM AVIATION SERIES

No. S18
(VOL. 2)

Vickers Supermarine Spitfire Mk.XVI, GC II/5,
French Air Force. Hanoi, French Indo-China 1947–1948. Serial unknown.

50 FIGHTERS 1939-1945

**Illustrated
and compiled by
Richard Ward**

ACKNOWLEDGEMENTS

This series of books covering fighter aircraft of the 1938–1945 period, of which this is the second volume, will illustrate the good, the bad and the indifferent, the well known and the little known, from one or two-off prototypes to 20,000 plus production runs. As in the first volume wherever possible new or little known photographs and colour schemes will be used to illustrate the well known types. Fighter aircraft of neutral countries and in post-war service will be illustrated in subsequent books as they have been in this volume. The aircraft have been arranged, with one or two exceptions, in alphabetical order by manuafcturer's name, chronologically within that name. My thanks to all those who assisted with information and photographs, especially Peter M. Bowers who has made available photographs of all American experimental types of the war years; for further information on these aircraft reference should be made to his two volumes *Forgotten Fighters*, 1 US Navy and 2 US Army.

Close-up detail of the sharkmouth of the Spitfire Mk.XVI
illustrated on the front cover and above. (ECA via J. Cuny)

Published by: Osprey Publishing Limited, England
Editorial Office: P.O. Box 5, Canterbury, Kent, England
Subscription & Business Office: P.O. Box 25, 707 Oxford Road, Reading, Berkshire, England

 ISBN 0 85045 201 5

Bell XP–77
USAAF

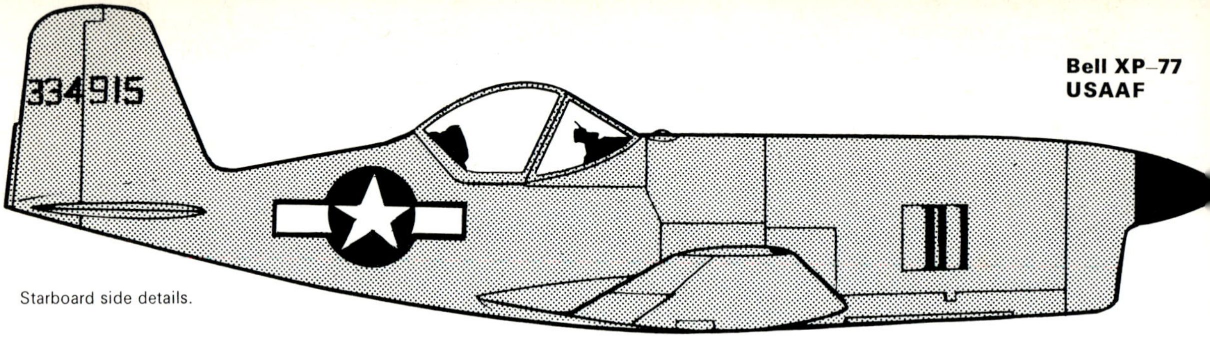

Starboard side details.

Span: 27ft. 6in. **Length:** 22ft. 11in. **Height:** 8ft. 2½in.
Engine: Ranger XV–770–7 12-cylinder air-cooled inverted V of 520hp.
Armament: 2×.5 machine guns plus an external bomb load up to 325lb.
Max. speed: 331mph at 4,000ft.
Weight: Empty 2,856lb. Loaded 3,670lb.

Silver Dope

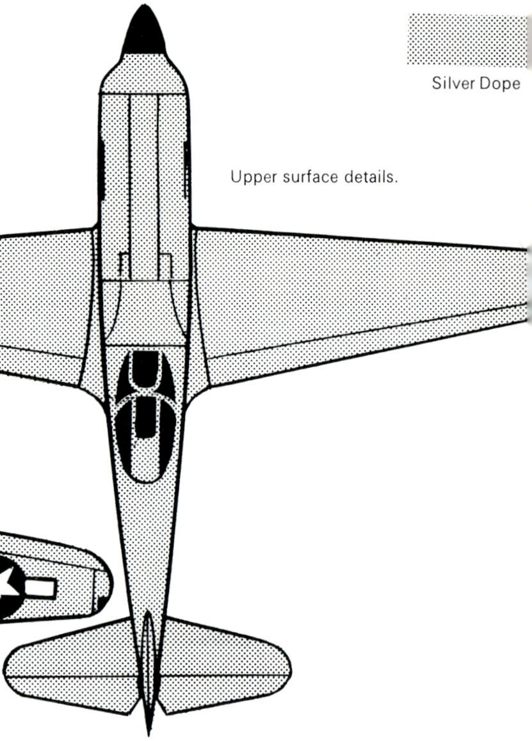

Upper surface details.

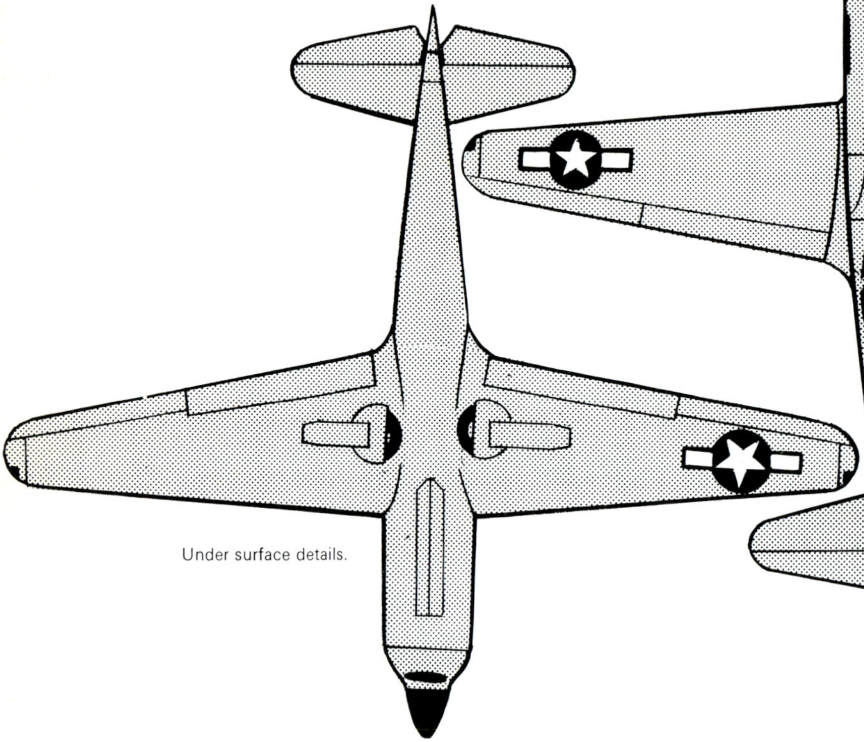

Under surface details.

Originally conceived in 1941, the first resin-bonded laminated wood XP–77 first flew in early 1944. Designed as a lightweight fighter utilising non-strategic materials in construction the aircraft was not a successful design and the development contract was cancelled in December 1944. Two prototypes were built and flown, the second one crashing at Eglin Field, the photograph illustrates the first aircraft with additional paintwork which included olive drab anti-glare panel and under surfaces, black lettering, striping and cockpit frames. (Peter M. Bowers)

Rocket-armed North American P–51D Mustang of the AURI photographed in 1970, flown as H–324 by the Netherlands East Indies Air Force during the closing months of World War II and in the post-war years until being handed over in 1947 to the newly-formed Indonesian Air Force when the code was changed to F–324. The USAAF serial was 4484473. (Hugo Hooftman)

50 FIGHTERS 1938-1945

This, the second volume covering fighter aircraft built between the years 1938 to 1945 extends the scope of the series by including some of those types of the period which saw service during the post-war years in many of the world's air forces. In some instances many types were in continuous service through the fifties, the sixties and even into the seventies, though only one type can claim this distinction, the evergreen North American P–51D Mustang, to give it its wartime designation. The F–51D Mustang last fired its guns in anger, albeit in the ground-attack role in the Israeli Air Force during the Sinai Campaign of 1956, it still flies with the AURI and with a few of the smaller South American air forces; illustrated in this book are two AURI Mustangs which saw action in the closing months of World War II with the Netherlands East Indies Air Force passing to the AURI on the formation of that force to continue in service for two decades in various roles, F–324 being photographed in 1970.

A rare type illustrated in this volume, with even rarer national markings is the IAR 81 two-seat fighter trainer conversion of the Royal Rumanian Air Force with roundel duplicated on the fin and rudder. Probably the IAR 80/81 series of fighters will attract the attention of one of the many producers of vacuum-formed kits in the not-too-distant future, as a model of this fighter would be a welcome addition to any collection of historic fighters.

As in the first volume this one also contains a quota of one or two-off prototypes and limited production aircraft, one example being the General Motors (Fisher Division) XP–75 and P–75 Eagle; it is unfortunate that this aircraft did not achieve operational status as it was basically an efficient airframe in its final configuration but powered by an undeveloped engine. The Eagle would have added a very interesting shape to the skies of World War II, again a good subject for the vacuum-formed kit.

Again a scheme is presented of the only high-wing monoplane fighter to see service in World War II together with one of the few biplanes to see first line service during that period.

Curtiss Mohawk Mk.IV
Royal Air Force

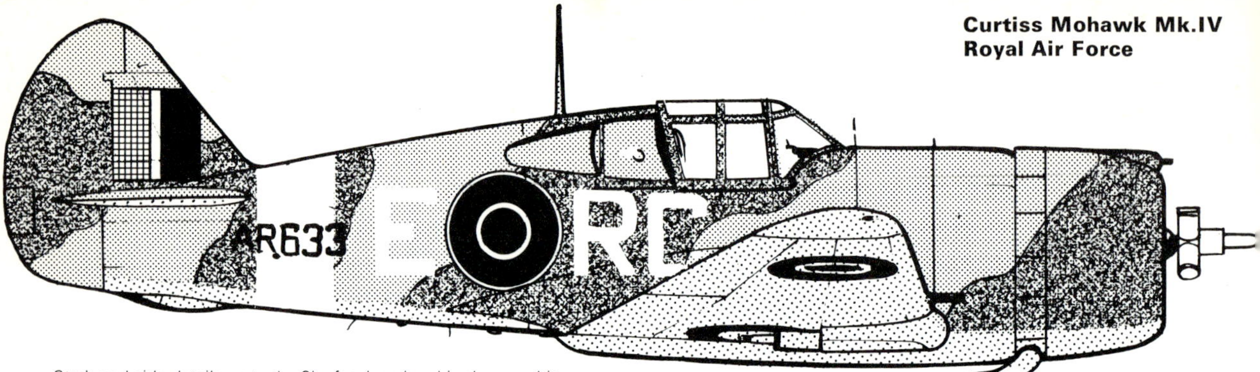

Starboard side details, note the Sky fuselage band is shown white.

Under surface details.

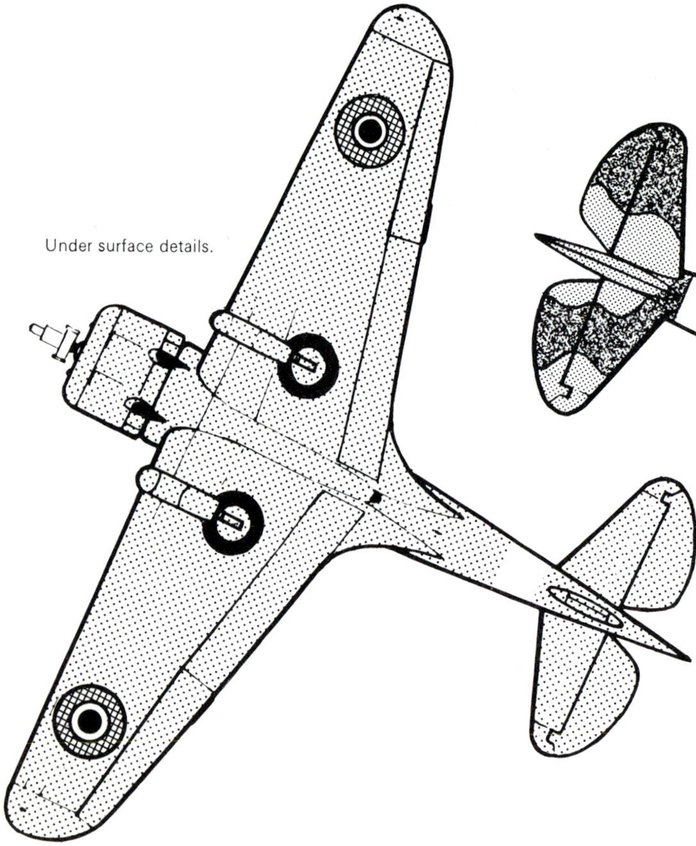

Upper surface details.

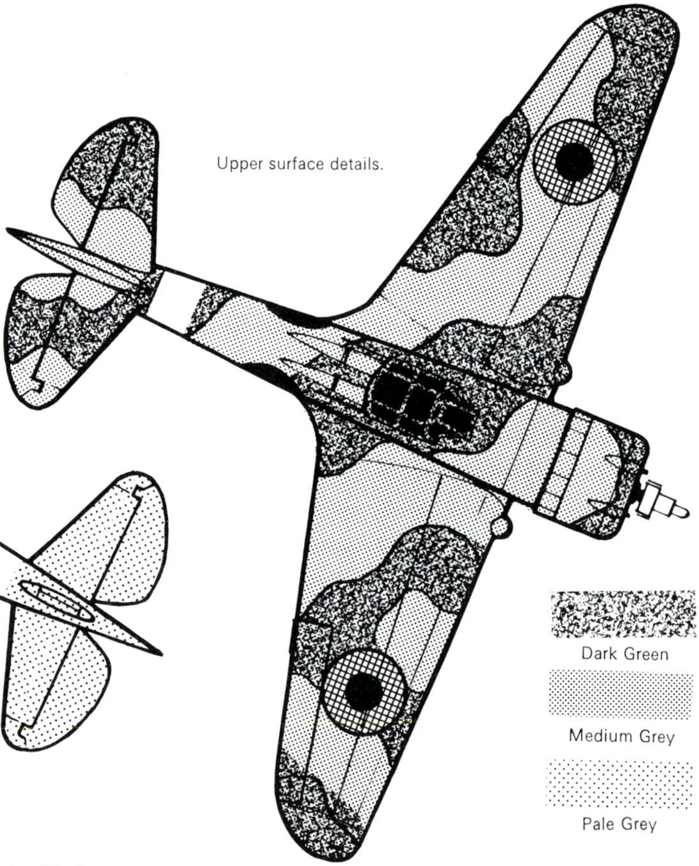

Span: 37ft. 4in **Length:** 28ft. 6in. **Height:** 9ft. 6in.
Engine: Wright Cyclone GR–1820–G205A 9-cylinder radial air-cooled of 1,200hp.
Armament: 6×7.5mm Browning machine guns.
Max. speed: 325mph.
Weight: Empty 4,540lb. Loaded 5,752lb.

Mohawk Mk.IV of No. 25 Fighter Leader School (FLS), RAF, The Mohawk was never operated in first line fighter units by the RAF in England, though No. 5 Squadron did fly the type in the Far East from December 1941 to June 1943. The majority of Mohawks delivered to the RAF after the fall of France were shipped to India and South Africa, those remaining in England being used by training and other units. (via Danny Morris)

Curtiss YP–37
USAAF

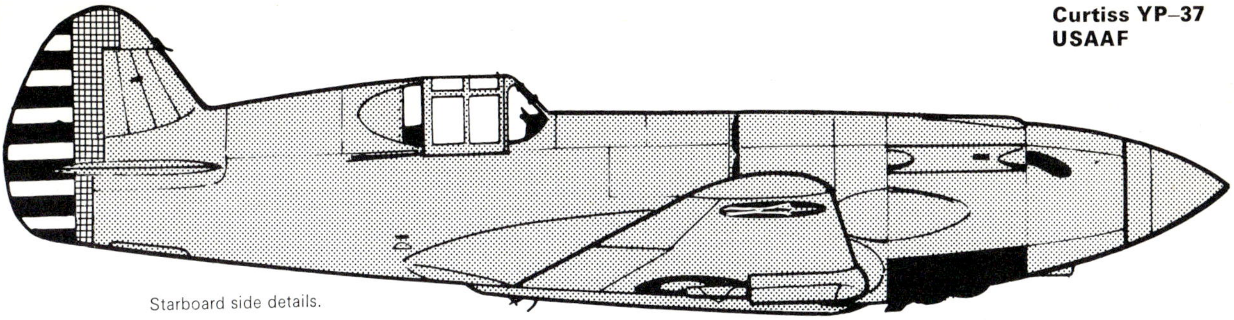

Starboard side details.

Under surface details.

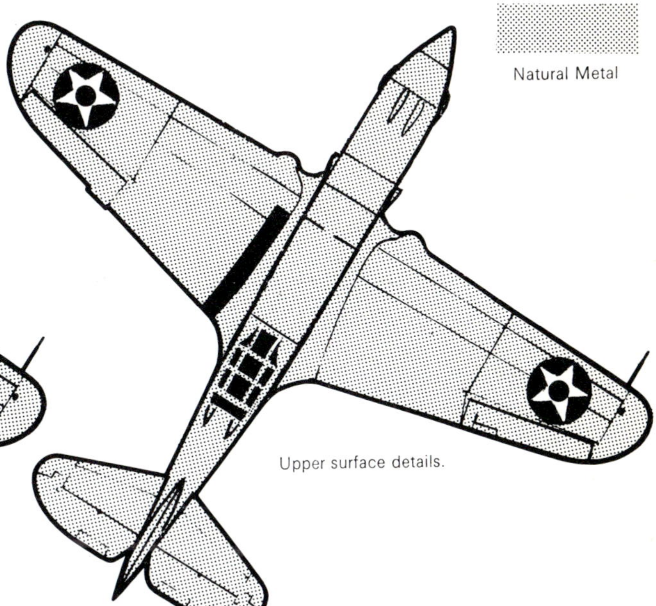

Upper surface details.

Natural Metal

The YP–37 was based on the earlier XP–37 which was the first American fighter type to exceed 300mph in 1937! Thirteen YP–37s were ordered in December 1937 but when the first of these were delivered in June 1939 the performance was so far below that guaranteed that the type was not put in production.

Span: 37ft. 4in. **Length:** 32ft. 10in. **Height:** 9ft. 6in.
Engine: Allison V–1710–12 12-cylinder liquid-cooled V of 1,000hp.
Armament: 1× .3in and 1× .5in. machine gun
Max. speed: 331mph.
Weight: Empty 5,723lb. Loaded 7,178lb.

Curtiss P–40C Tomahawk USAAF

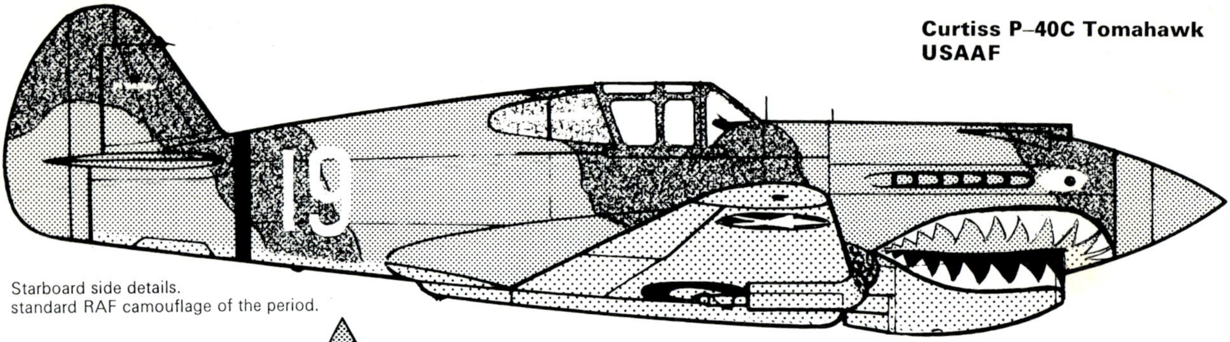

Starboard side details.
standard RAF camouflage of the period.

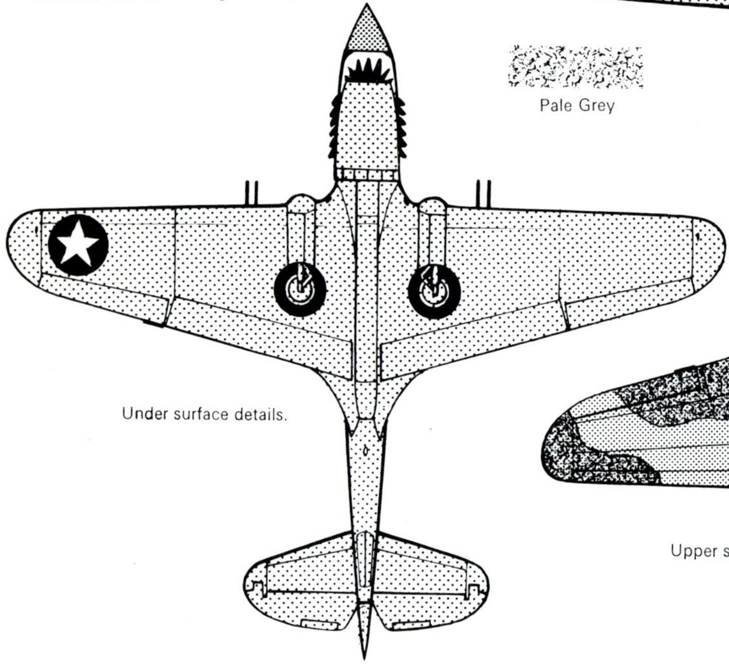

Under surface details.

Pale Grey

Dark Green

Dark Earth

Pale Blue

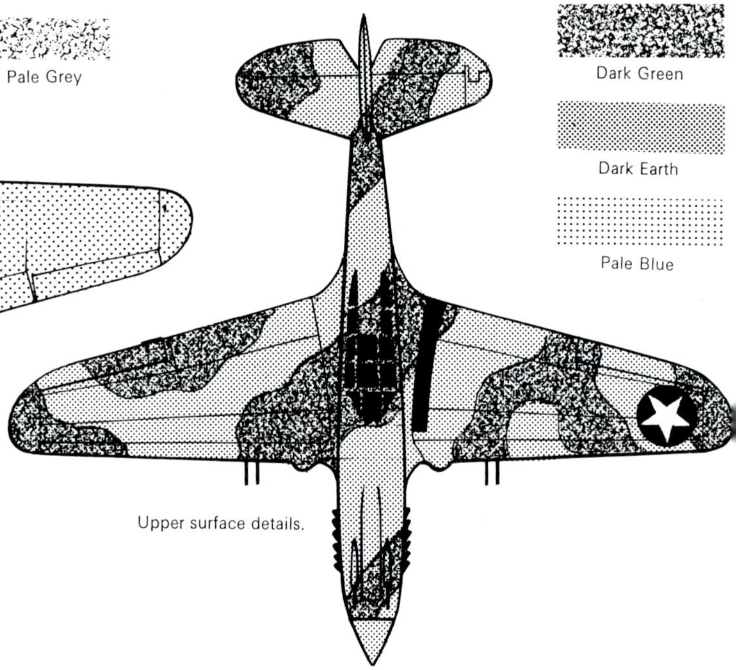

Upper surface details.

Span: 37ft. 4in. **Length:** 31ft. 9in.
Height: 12ft. 4in.
Engine: Allison V–1710–33 12-cylinder liquid-cooled V of 1040hp.
Armament: 2×.5in machine guns mounted above engine plus 4×.3in in wings.
Max. speed: 345mph.
Weight: Empty 5,8121lb.
Loaded 7,550/8,058lb.

Tomahawk 74 coming into land at Kunming some time in 1942, note the two eyes on the engine cowl due to a panel change with another aircraft, 74 is the second aircraft in the line-up below, note yellow and white design on wheel disc, red, yellow and white on 19. (USAF)

Line-up of Curtiss P–40C Tomahawks of the 23rd Fighter Group on Kunming airfield, China early in 1942. This unit was prior to induction into the USAAF the American Volunteer Group popularly known as the Flying Tigers under the command of General Chennault. 100 Tomahawks of a British Purchasing Commission order awaiting delivery to the UK were relinquished in favour of the Chinese, 90 of these aircraft formed the initial equipment of the AVG hence the RAF camouflage.

Curtiss XP–40Q Warhawk
USAAF

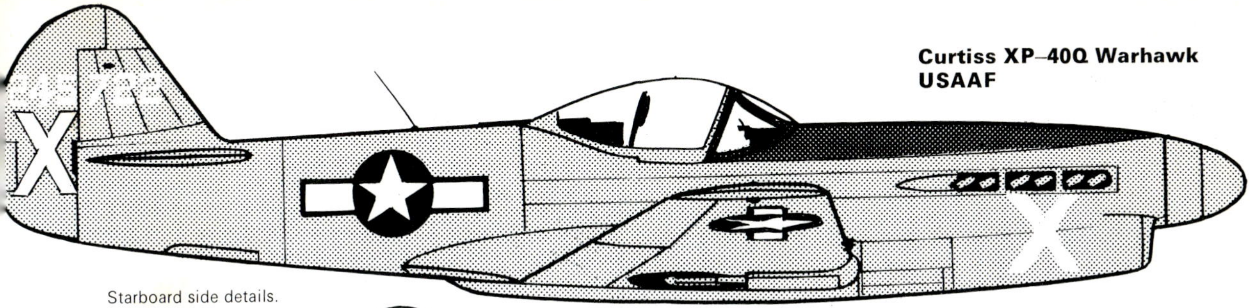

Starboard side details.

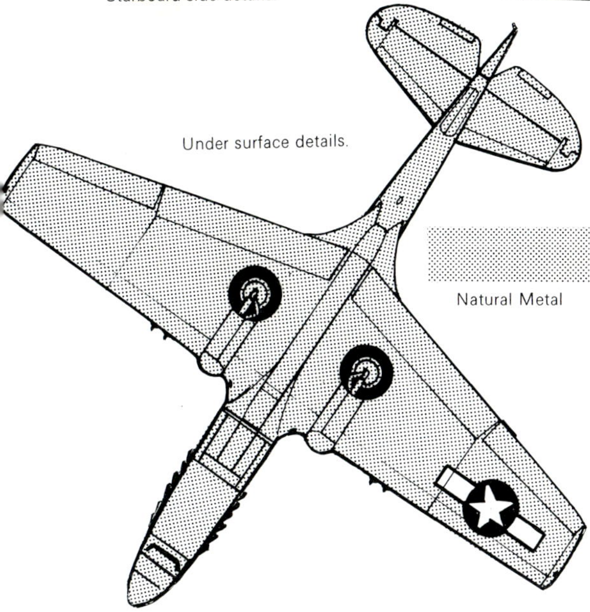

Under surface details.

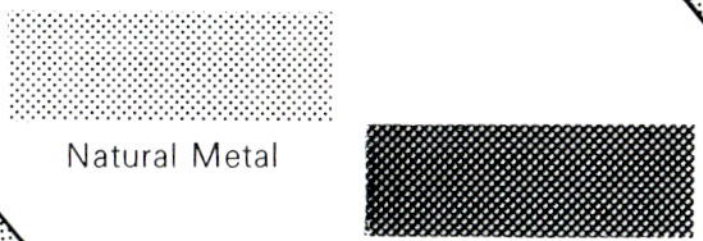

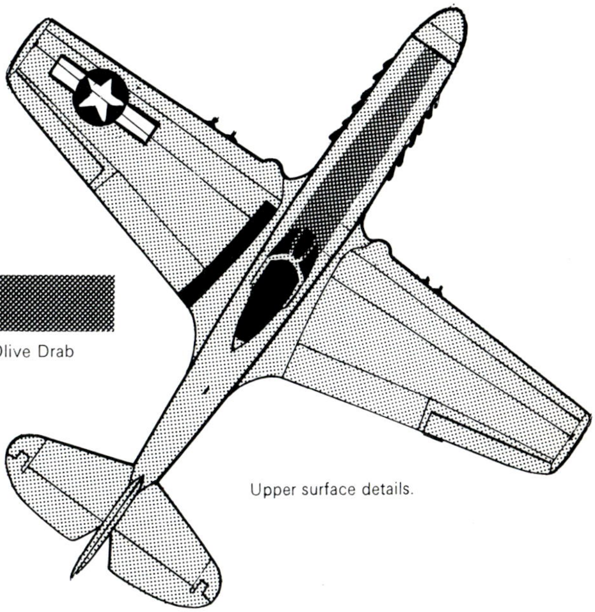

Upper surface details.

Span: 35ft. 3in. **Length:** 35ft. 4in. **Height:** 12ft. 4in.
Engine: Allison V–1710–121 12-cylinder liquid-cooled V of 1425hp.
Armament: 4×.5in machine guns.
Max. speed: 422mph.
Weight: Empty Loaded 9,000lb.

The XP–40Q represented the last attempt by Curtiss to bring the performance of the Warhawk into line with the P–51 and P–47, though many modifications were made to the airframe, armament reduced to 4×.5in machine guns and a bubble canopy fitted, performance still fell short of the P–51 and P–47 with the result the last of the Warhawks did not reach production. Top photo shows the second Q 245722 and the lower the third 324574, note different canopy. (Peter M. Bowers)

Curtiss XP–46
USAAF

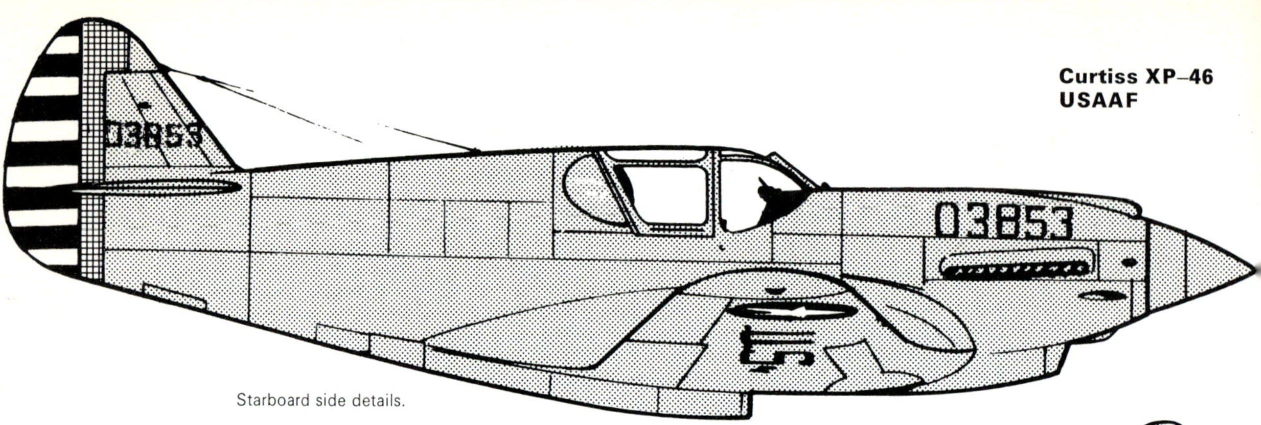

Starboard side details.

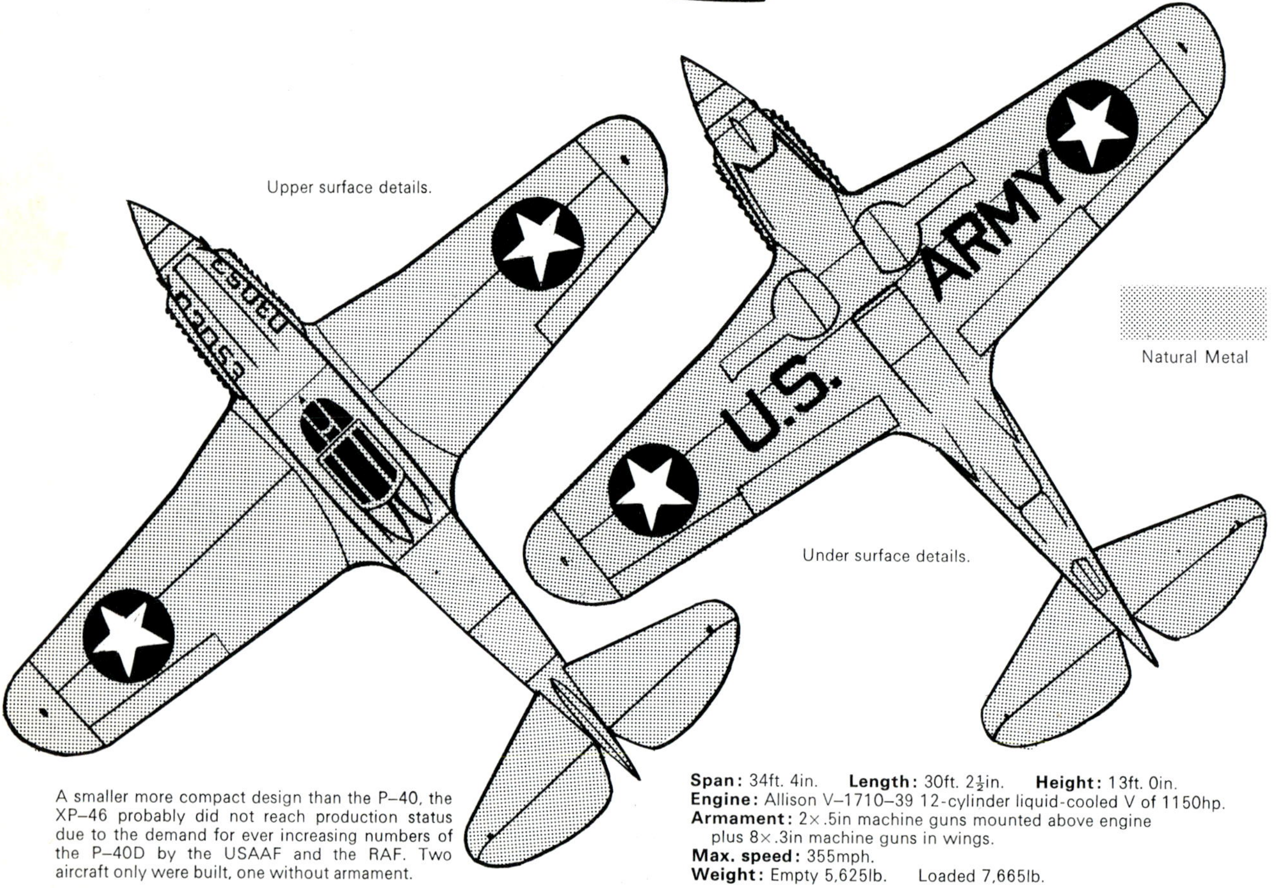

Upper surface details.

Under surface details.

Natural Metal

A smaller more compact design than the P–40, the XP–46 probably did not reach production status due to the demand for ever increasing numbers of the P–40D by the USAAF and the RAF. Two aircraft only were built, one without armament.

Span: 34ft. 4in. **Length:** 30ft. 2½in. **Height:** 13ft. 0in.
Engine: Allison V–1710–39 12-cylinder liquid-cooled V of 1150hp.
Armament: 2×.5in machine guns mounted above engine plus 8×.3in machine guns in wings.
Max. speed: 355mph.
Weight: Empty 5,625lb. Loaded 7,665lb.

Curtiss XP–60C
USAAF

Starboard side details.

Span: 41ft. 4in. **Length:** 33ft. 10in. **Height:** 15ft. 0in.
Engine: Pratt and Whitney R–2800–53 18-cylinder air-cooled radial of 2000hp.
Armament: 4×.5in machine guns.
Max. speed: 414 mph.
Weight: Empty 8,600lb. Loaded 10,785lb.

Olive Drab

Pale Grey

Under surface details.

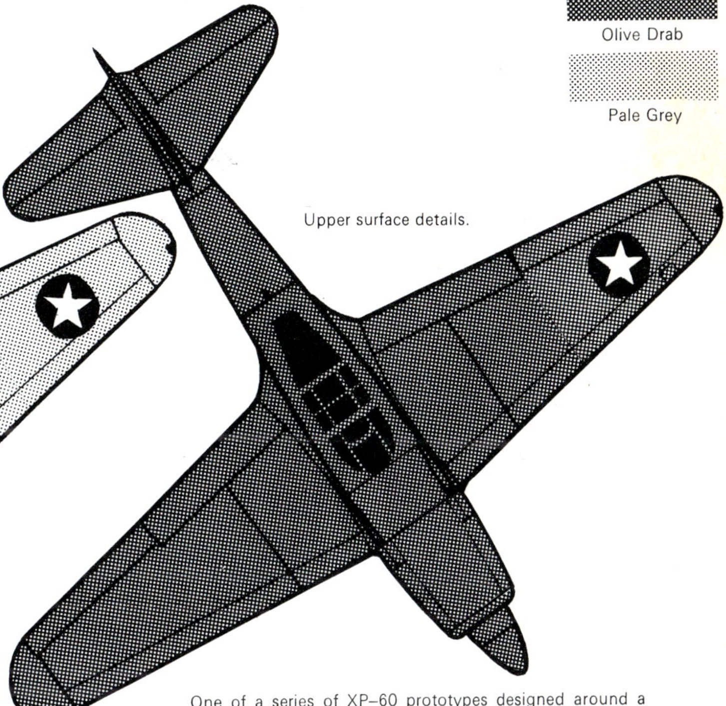

Upper surface details.

One of a series of XP–60 prototypes designed around a variety of engines. The XP–60C was originally intended to have the 16-cylinder Chrysler XIV–2220 fitted but was eventually completed with an R–2800–53 driving contra-rotating airscrews. The aircraft made a poor showing at the fighter trials held at Patterson Field in April 1943 with the result it did not go into production. (Peter M. Bowers)

Curtiss YP–60E
USAAF

Span: 41ft. 4in. **Length:** 33ft. 10in. **Height:** 15ft. 0in.
Engine: Pratt and Whitney R–2800–10 18-cylinder air-cooled radial of 2100hp.
Armament: 6×.5in machine guns.
Max. speed: 405 mph.
Weight: Empty 8,285lb. Loaded 11,523lb.

Natural Metal

Olive Drab

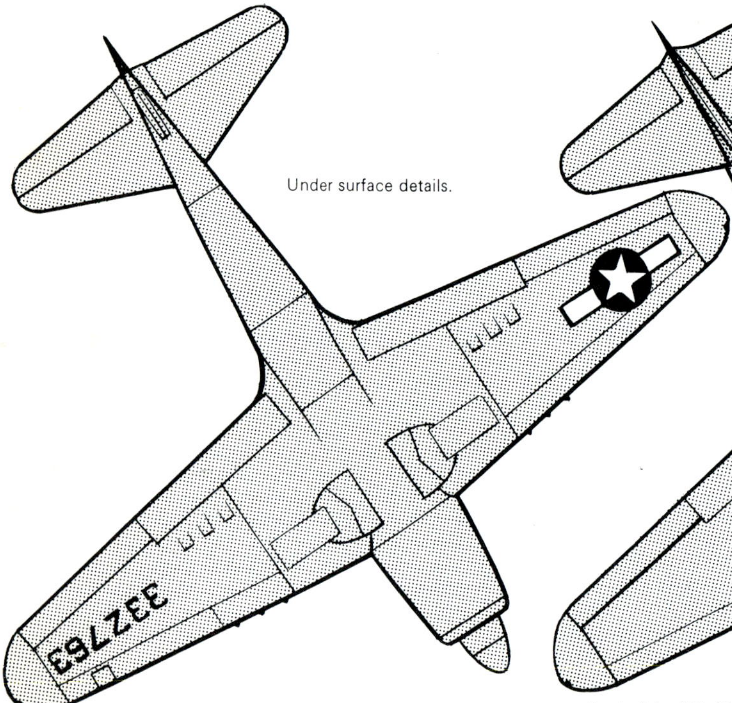

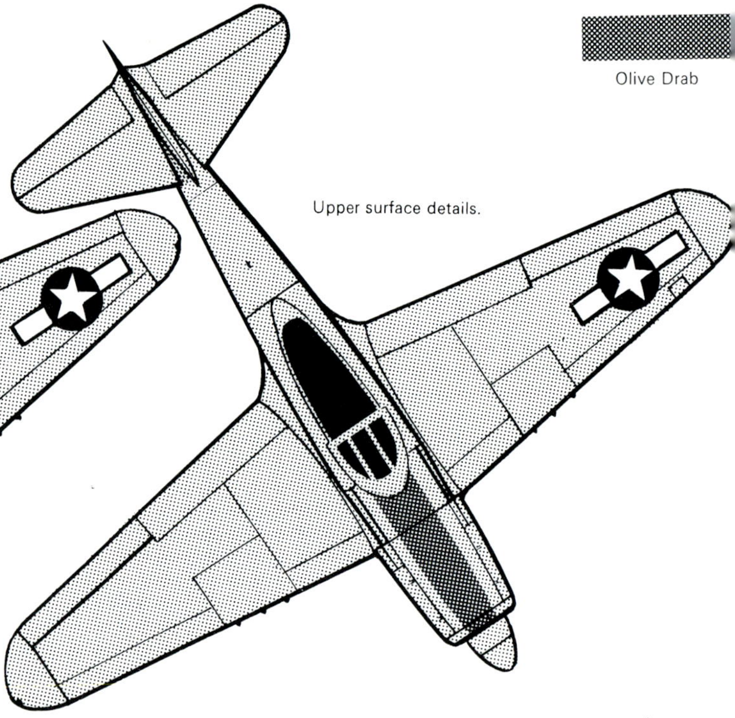

Last of the XP–60 series of prototypes, the R–2800–18 powered YP–60E with cut down rear fuselage and bubble canopy looked very similar to the P–47D but could not match the Thunderbolt's performance and became another fighter which did not quite make it. (Peter M. Bowers)

Port and starboard views of the Fw 190F–8 flown by the Gruppenadjutant of 2/SG 2 "Immelmann", Hungary, winter 1944–45. Note the wheel covers have been removed. (Hans Obert)

Focke-Wulf Fw 190F–8
Luftwaffe

Pale Blue Grey
White on Grey
Yellow

Span: 34ft. 5in.
Length: 29ft. 4½in.
Height: 13ft. 0in.
Engine: BMW 801D–2 14-cylinder air-cooled radial of 1,700hp.
Armament: 2×7.9mm MG 17 machine guns mounted to fire through the airscrew plus 2×20mm MG 151 cannon mounted in wing roots also firing through the airscrew.
Max. speed: 394 mph.
Weight: Empty 7,330lb. Loaded with external stores 10,850lb.

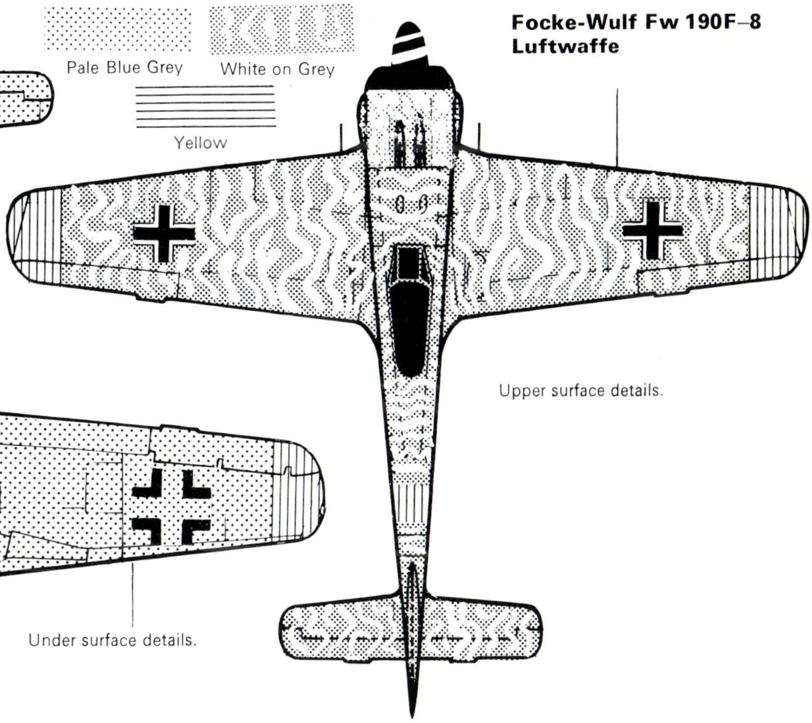

Upper surface details.

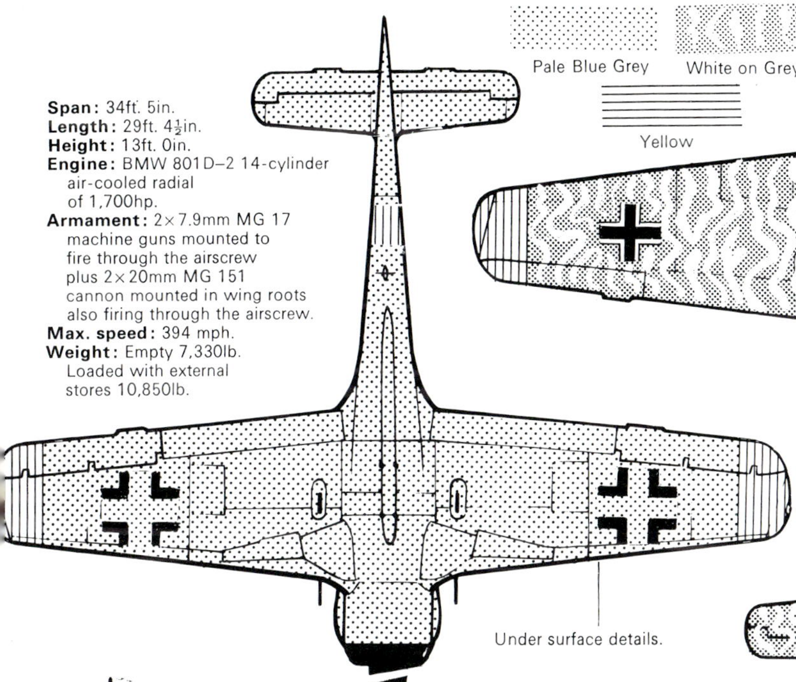

Under surface details.

Starboard side details.

Grumman F6F–5 Hellcat
US Navy

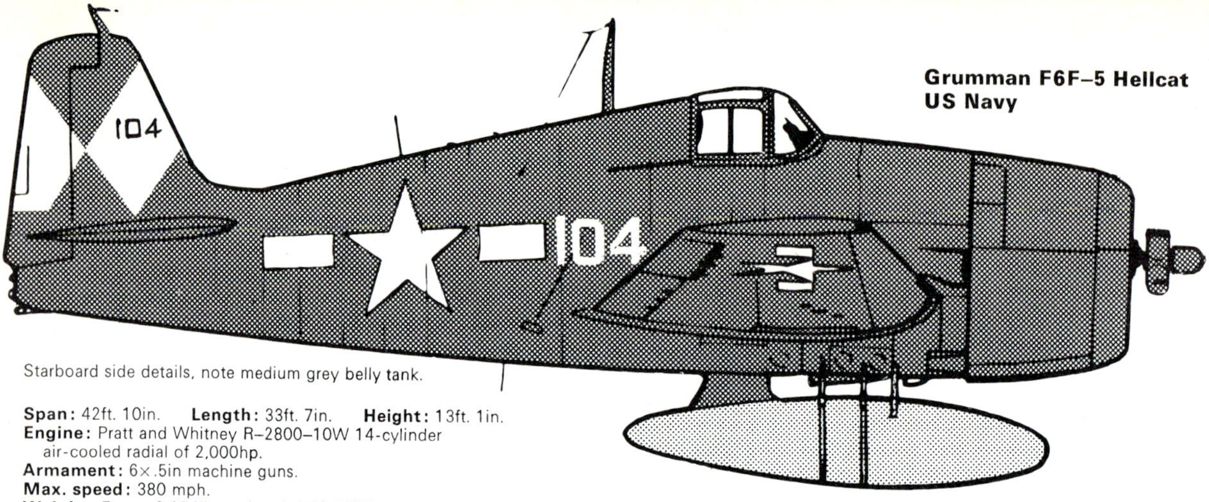

Starboard side details, note medium grey belly tank.

Span: 42ft. 10in. **Length:** 33ft. 7in. **Height:** 13ft. 1in.
Engine: Pratt and Whitney R–2800–10W 14-cylinder air-cooled radial of 2,000hp.
Armament: 6×.5in machine guns.
Max. speed: 380 mph.
Weight: Empty 9,154lb. Loaded 12,500lb.

Sea Blue

Undercarriage door, port and starboard.

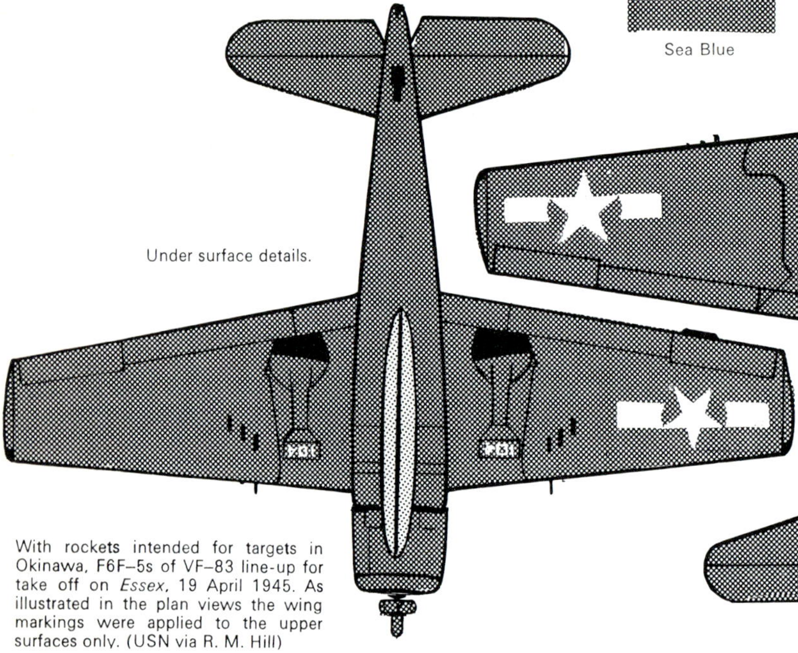

Under surface details.

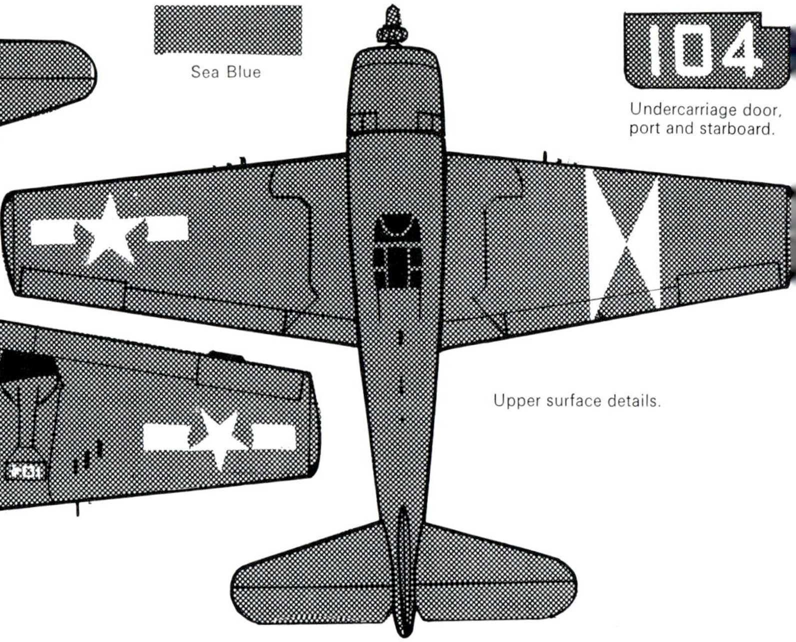

Upper surface details.

With rockets intended for targets in Okinawa, F6F–5s of VF–83 line-up for take off on *Essex*, 19 April 1945. As illustrated in the plan views the wing markings were applied to the upper surfaces only. (USN via R. M. Hill)

General Motors (Fisher) XP–75/P–75 Eagle USAAF

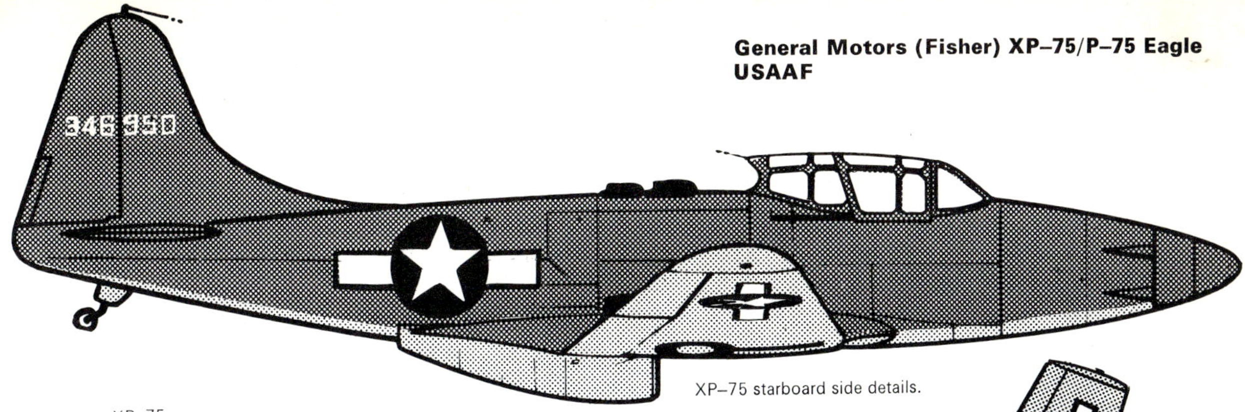

XP–75 starboard side details.

XP–75 upper surface detail, under surface identical in pale grey.

P–75 under surface details.

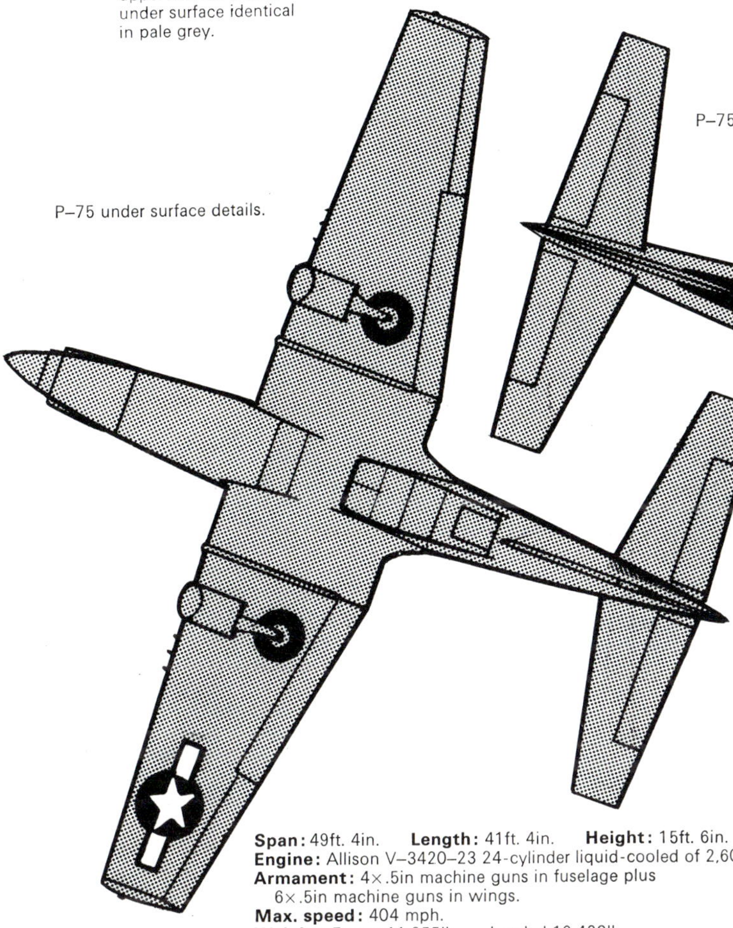

P–75 upper surface details.

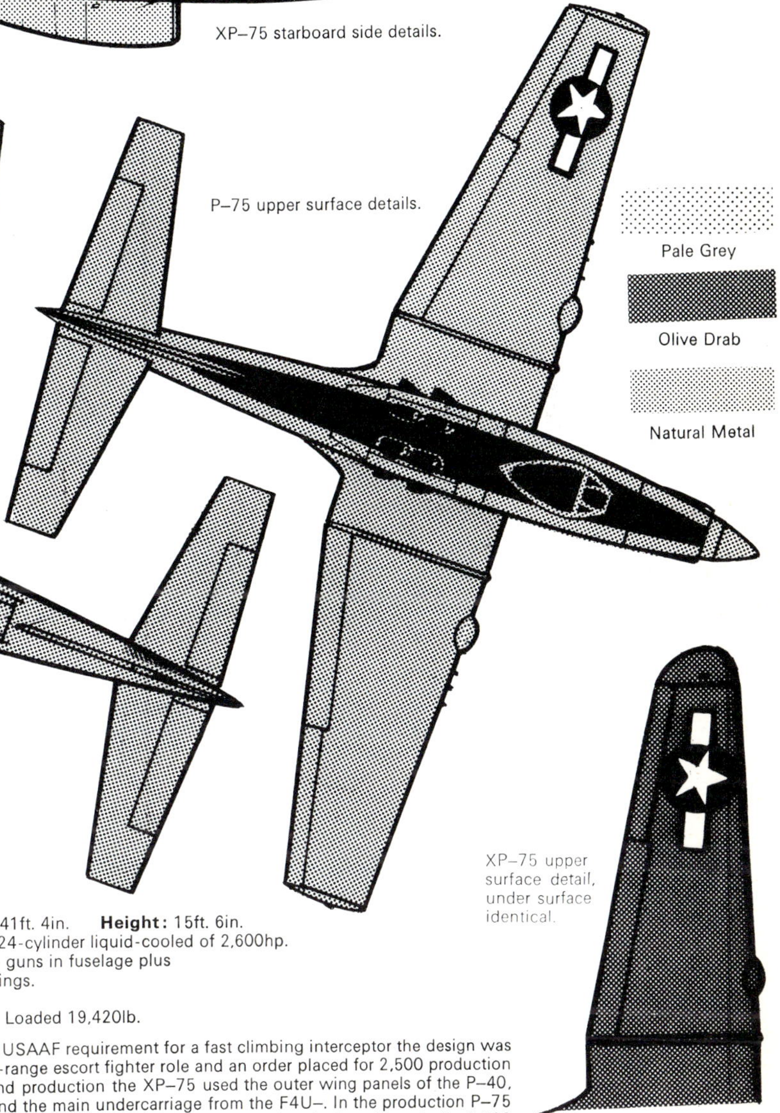

XP–75 upper surface detail, under surface identical.

Span: 49ft. 4in. **Length:** 41ft. 4in. **Height:** 15ft. 6in.
Engine: Allison V–3420–23 24-cylinder liquid-cooled of 2,600hp.
Armament: 4×.5in machine guns in fuselage plus 6×.5in machine guns in wings.
Max. speed: 404 mph.
Weight: Empty 11,255lb. Loaded 19,420lb.

Designed and built to a 1942 USAAF requirement for a fast climbing interceptor the design was modified in 1943 for the long-range escort fighter role and an order placed for 2,500 production aircraft. To facilitate design and production the XP–75 used the outer wing panels of the P–40, the tail unit from the A–24 and the main undercarriage from the F4U–. In the production P–75 a redesigned tail unit was fitted. Six production P–75s were completed when the order for 2,500 aircraft was cancelled mainly due to the excellence of the long-range capabilities of the P–51 and P–47. For photographs see inside back cover.

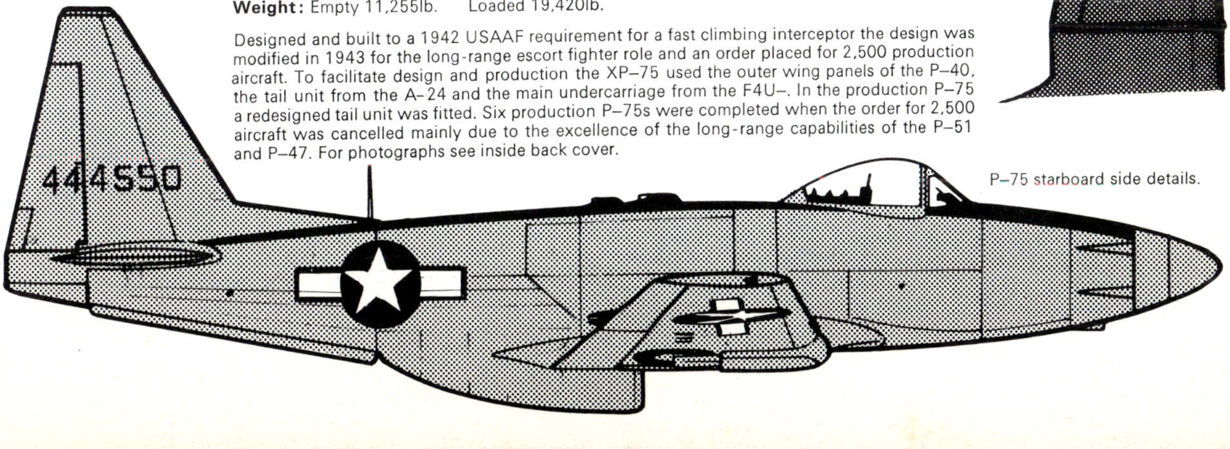

P–75 starboard side details.

Hawker Typhoon Ib
Royal Canadian Air Force

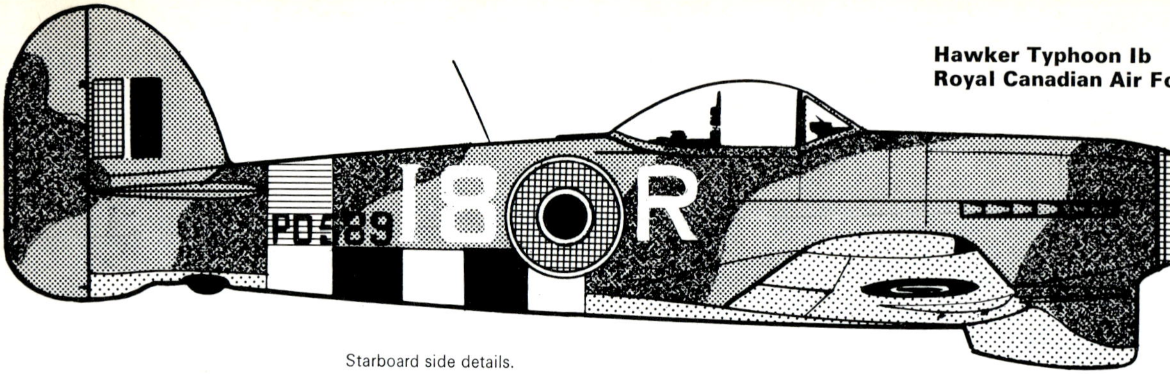

Starboard side details.

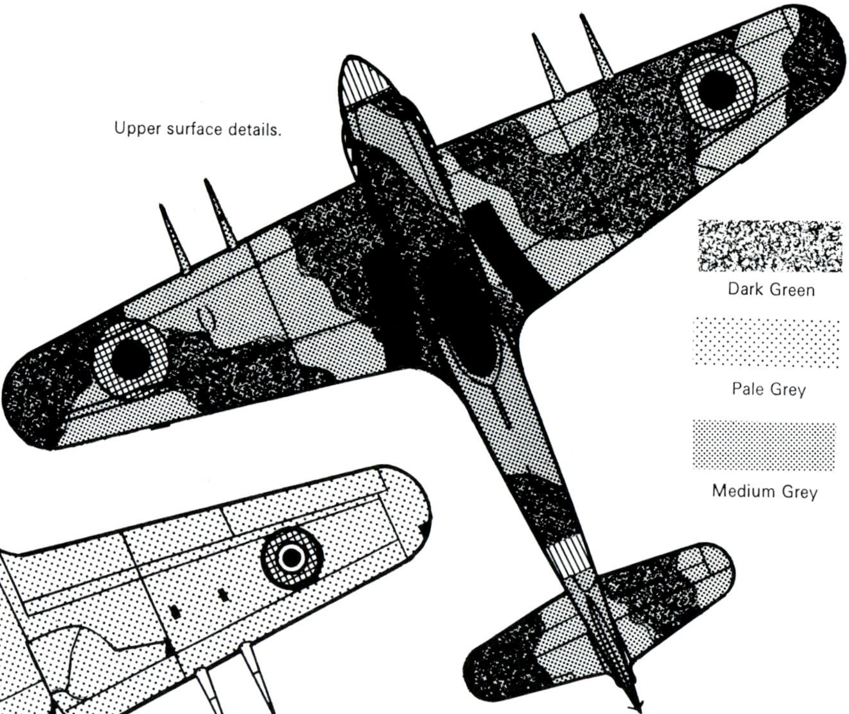

Upper surface details.

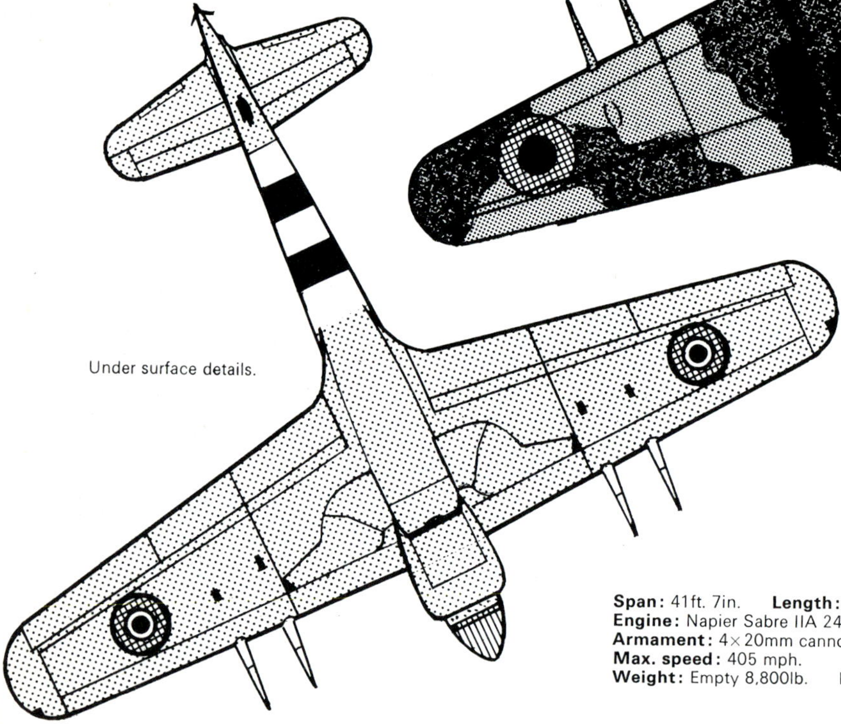

Under surface details.

Span: 41ft. 7in. **Length:** 31ft. 10in. **Height:** 16ft. 3in.
Engine: Napier Sabre IIA 24-cylinder horizontal H liquid-cooled of 2,180hp.
Armament: 4×20mm cannon plus 2×1,000lb bombs or 8×60lb RPs.
Max. speed: 405 mph.
Weight: Empty 8,800lb. Loaded 11,400lb.

Typhoon Ib of No. 440 Squadron, 2nd TAF, waiting to be re-armed on a Dutch airfield, autumn 1944.

Hawker Tempest V
Royal Air Force

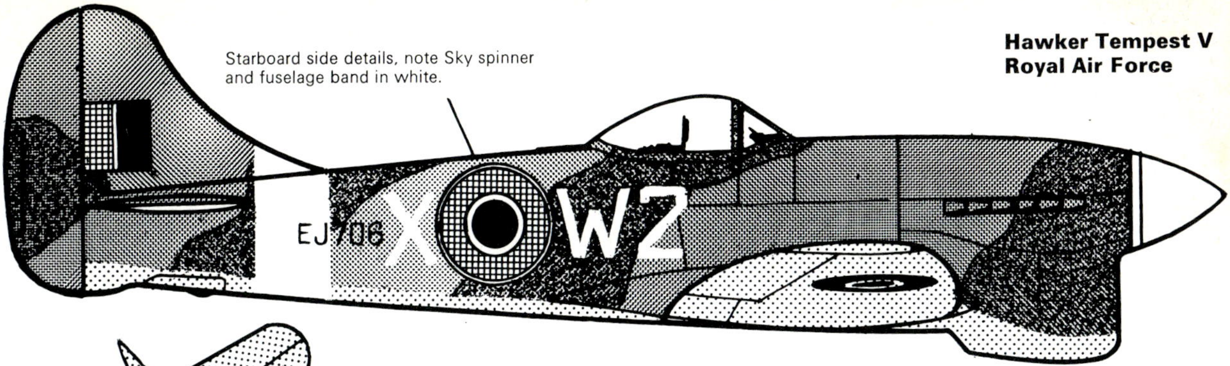

Starboard side details, note Sky spinner and fuselage band in white.

Span: 41ft. 0in. **Length:** 33ft. 8in. **Height:** 16ft. 0in.
Engine: Napier Sabre IIB 24-cylinder horizontal H liquid-cooled of 2,200hp.
Armament: 4× 20mm cannon plus 2× 1,000lb bombs or 8× 60lb RPs.
Max. speed: 435 mph.
Weight: Empty 9,250lb. Loaded 13,500lb.

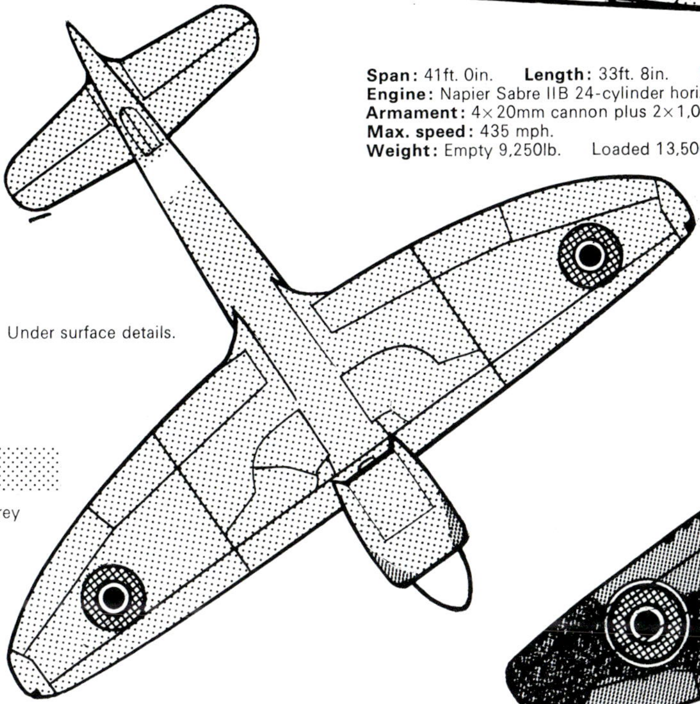

Under surface details.

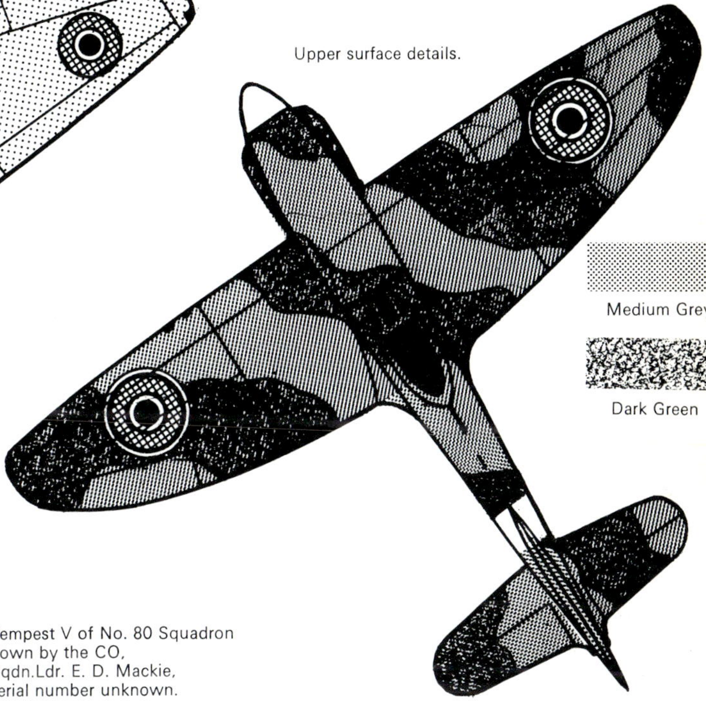

Upper surface details.

Pale Grey

Medium Grey

Dark Green

Tempest V of No. 80 Squadron flown by the CO, Sqdn.Ldr. E. D. Mackie, serial number unknown.

Hawker Tempest F.2
Royal Air Force

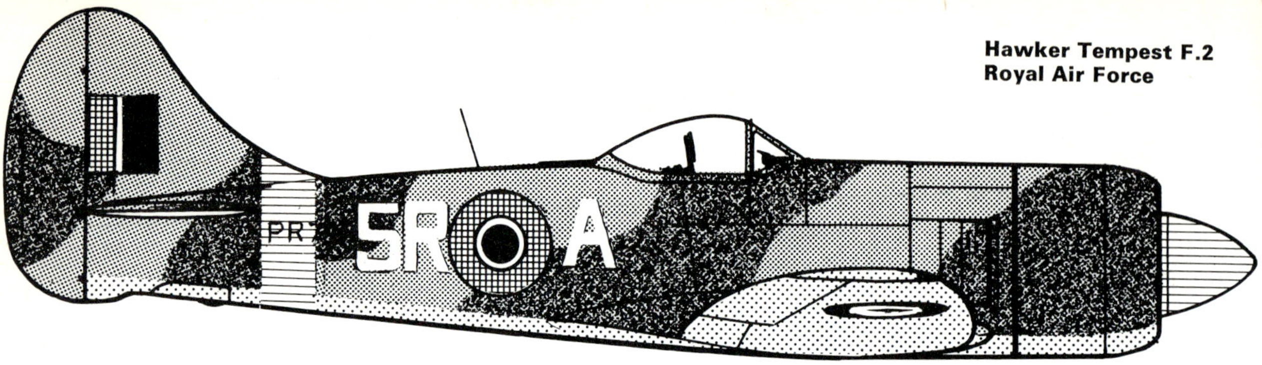

Starboard side details.

Span: 41ft. 0in. **Length:** 43ft. 5in. **Height:** 15ft. 6in.
Engine: Bristol Centaurus V 18-cylinder air-cooled radial of 2,520hp.
Armament: 4×20mm cannon plus 2×1,000lb bombs or 8×60lb RPs.
Max. speed: 422 mph.
Weight: Empty 9,300lb. Loaded 13,900lb.

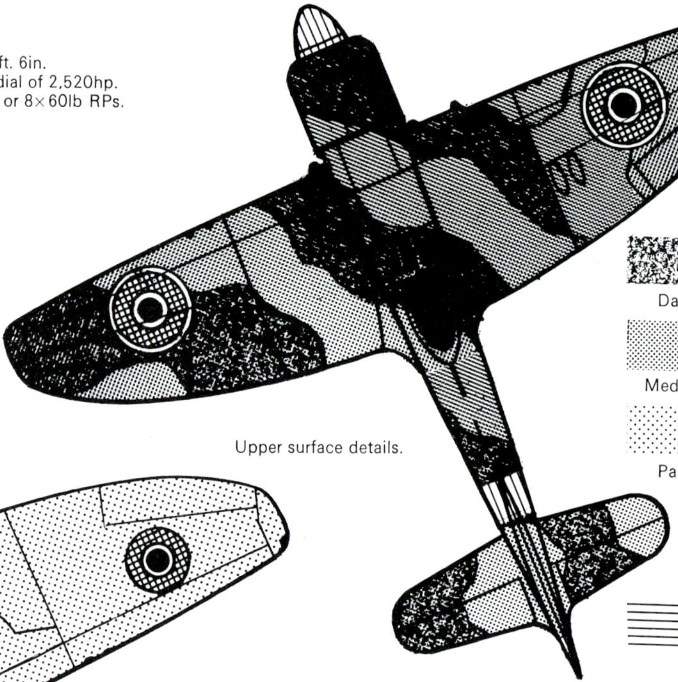

Upper surface details.

Dark Green
Medium Grey
Pale Grey
Sky

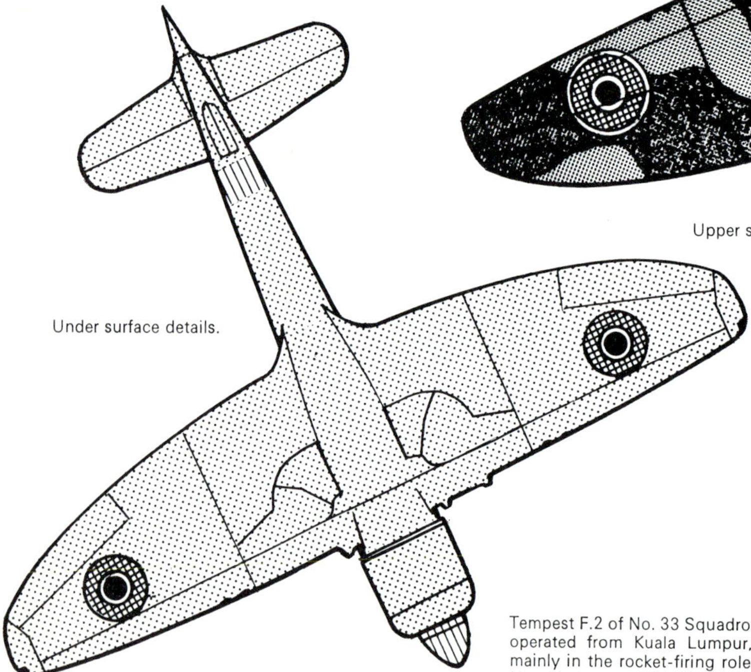

Under surface details.

Tempest F.2 of No. 33 Squadron when part of the Far East Air Force where the squadron operated from Kuala Lumpur, Butterworth and Penang on anti-terrorist operations mainly in the rocket-firing role winkling out well hidden Communist jungle hide-outs. No. 33 Squadron flew the Tempest II from 1946 to 1951 when it re-equipped with Hornet F.3s.

IAR 81
Royal Rumanian Air Force

Starboard side details.

Span: 32ft. 10in. **Length:** 26ft. 10in. **Height:** 11ft. 10in.
Engine: IAR Gnôme-Rhone 14K Mistral-Major 14-cylinder air-cooled radial of 940hp.
Armament: Unknown.
Max. speed: 318 mph approx.
Weight: Unknown.

Upper surface details.

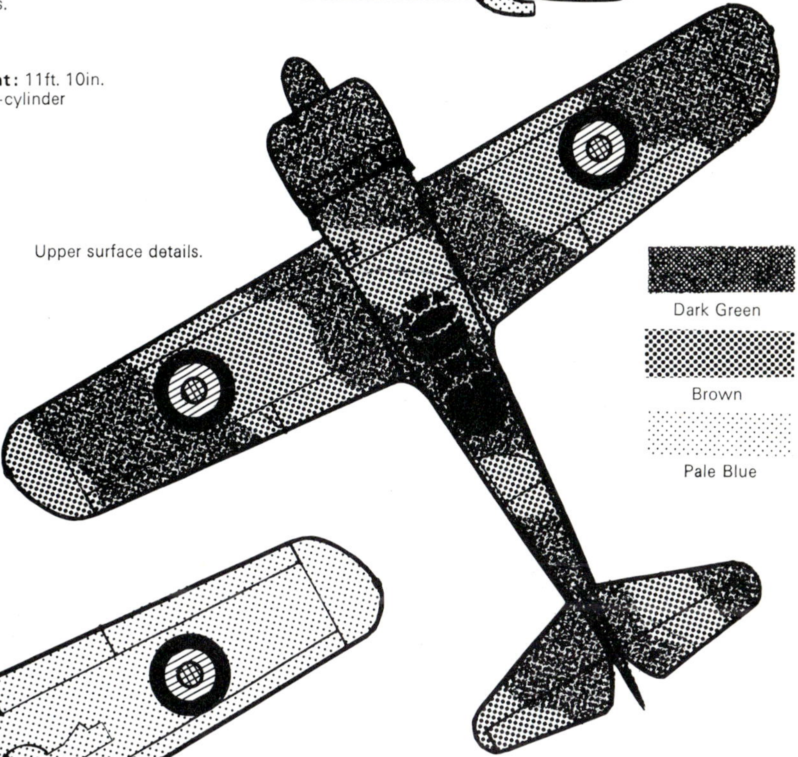

Under surface details.

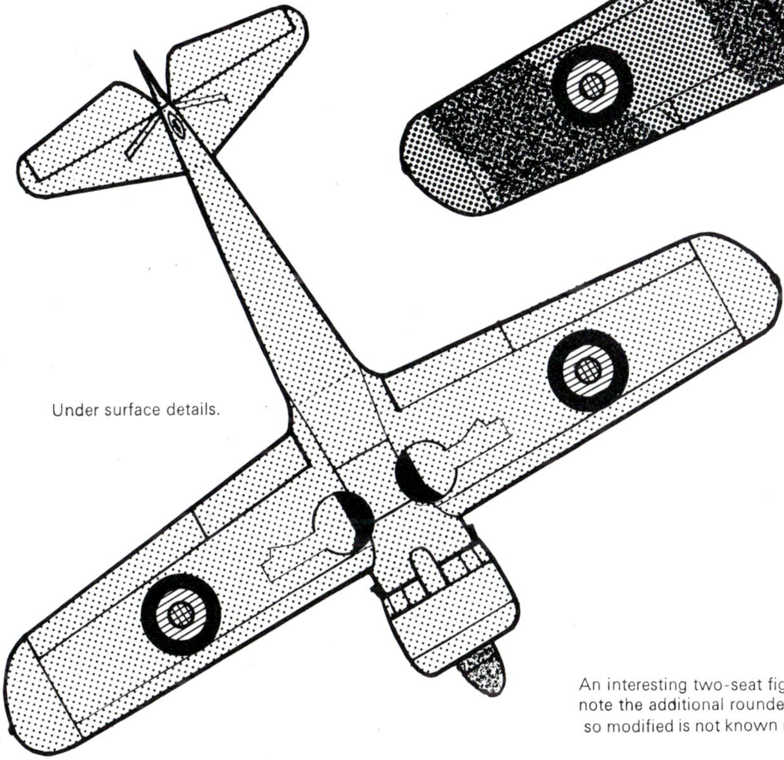

An interesting two-seat fighter trainer conversion from a standard IAR 81, note the additional roundel on the fin and rudder. How many aircraft were so modified is not known neither is the performance in this configuration.

I–17
Russian Air Force

Starboard side details.

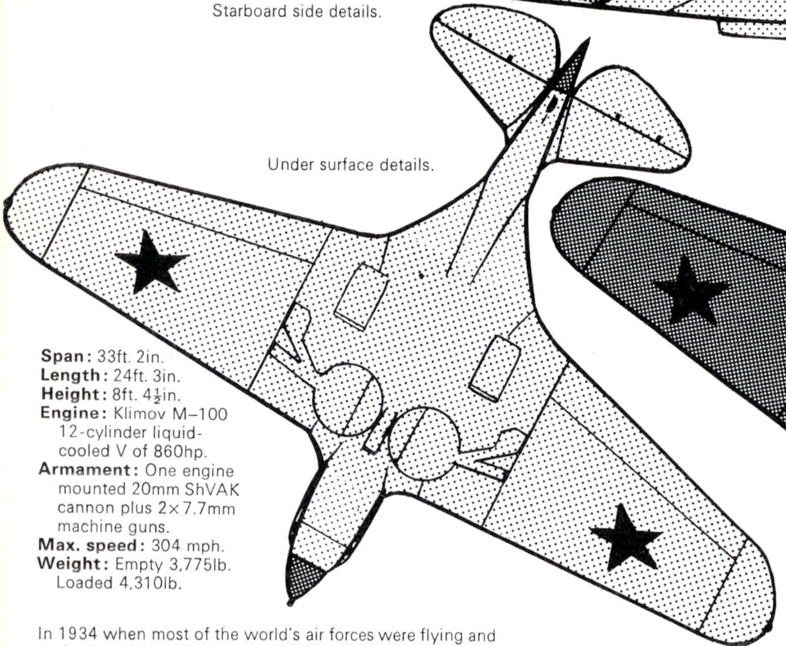

Under surface details.

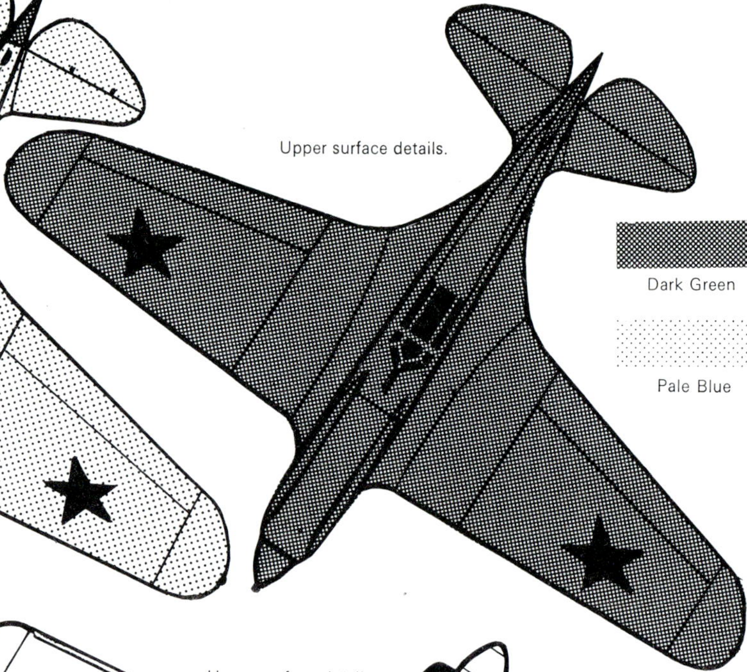

Upper surface details.

Dark Green

Pale Blue

Span: 33ft. 2in.
Length: 24ft. 3in.
Height: 8ft. $4\frac{1}{2}$in.
Engine: Klimov M–100 12-cylinder liquid-cooled V of 860hp.
Armament: One engine mounted 20mm ShVAK cannon plus 2×7.7mm machine guns.
Max. speed: 304 mph.
Weight: Empty 3,775lb. Loaded 4,310lb.

In 1934 when most of the world's air forces were flying and designing biplane fighters the I–17 made its first flight, for its time a remarkably clean design with semi-retractable wing radiators, shown on the side-view illustration retracted. The I–17 was put into limited production in 1937 through 1939, it saw limited front-line service in the Russian East facing the Japanese during the various border incidents and later on the European Eastern Front from which it was withdrawn in 1942.

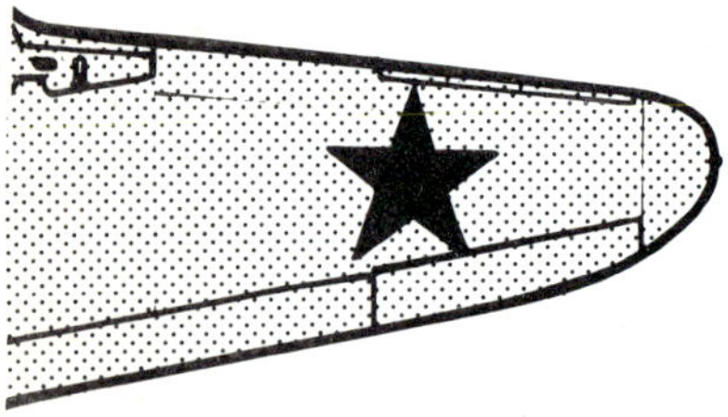

Under surface details.

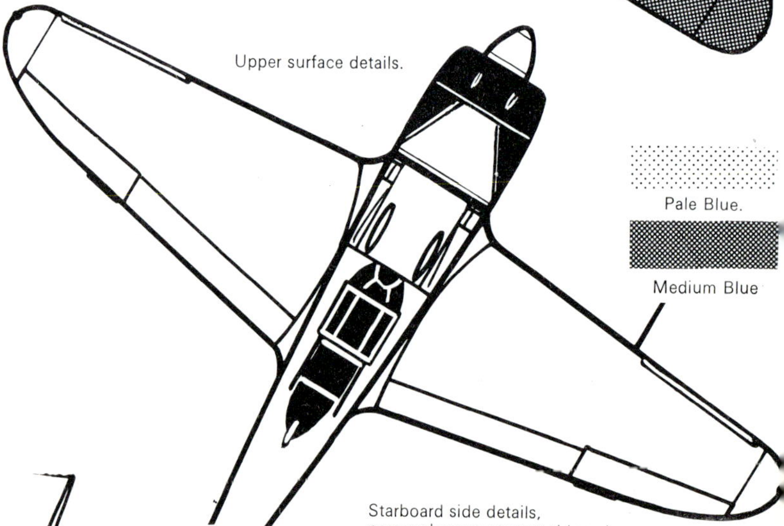

Upper surface details.

Pale Blue.

Medium Blue

Starboard side details, personal score on port side only, fuselage star thinly outlined with black.

Lavochkin La–7
Russian Air Force

La–7 flown by Ivan Kojedub during winter of 1945.

Macchi MC 205 Veltro
Aviazione Della RSI

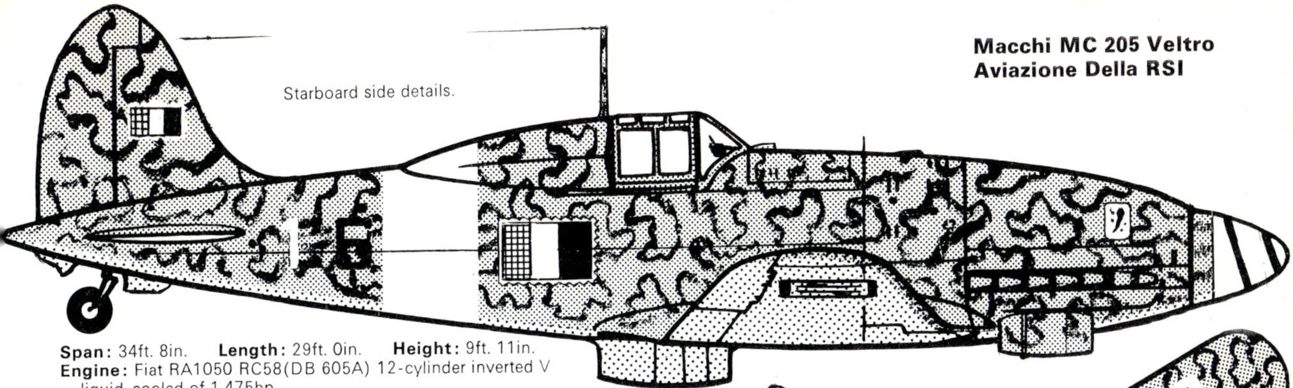

Starboard side details.

Span: 34ft. 8in. **Length:** 29ft. 0in. **Height:** 9ft. 11in.
Engine: Fiat RA1050 RC58(DB 605A) 12-cylinder inverted V liquid-cooled of 1,475hp.
Armament: 2×12.7mm machine guns plus 2×20mm Mauser MG 151 wing-mounted cannon.
Max. speed: 401 mph.
Weight: Empty 5,690lb. Loaded 7,515lb.

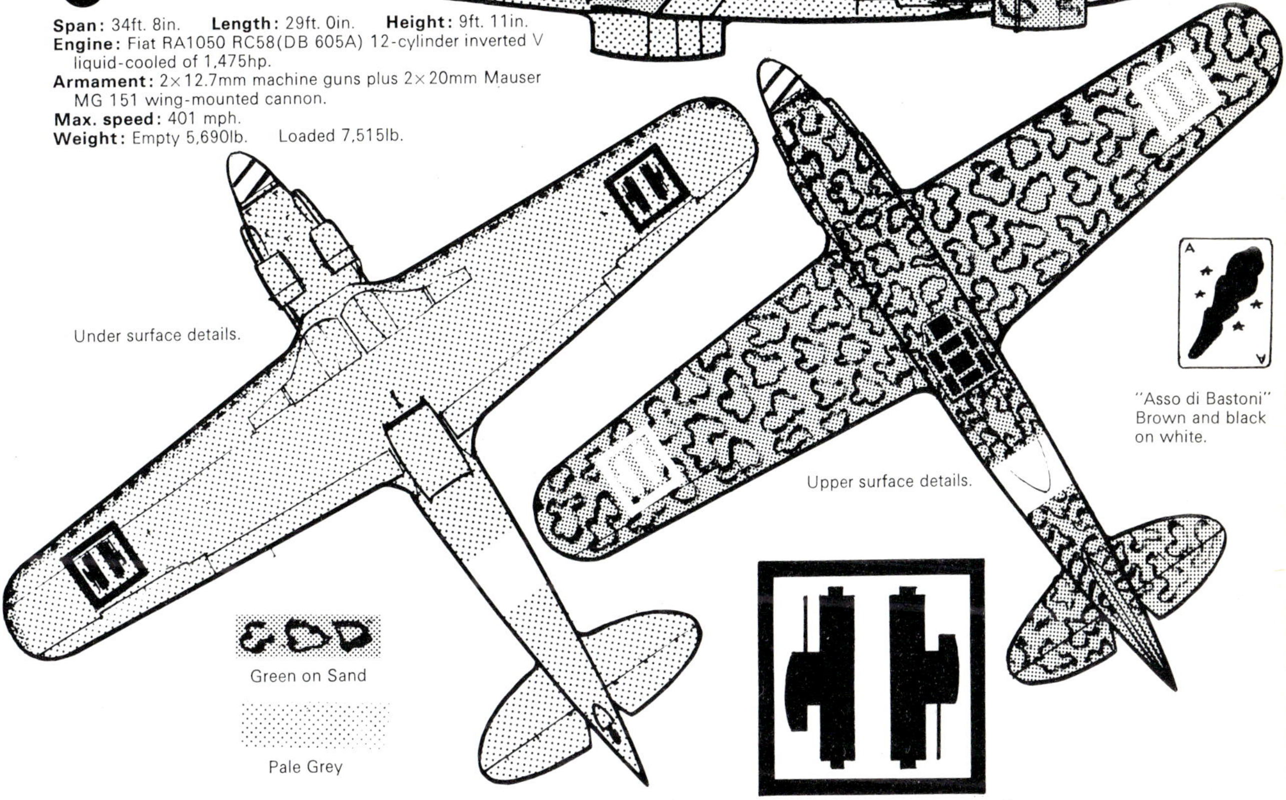

Under surface details.

Upper surface details.

"Asso di Bastoni" Brown and black on white.

Green on Sand

Pale Grey

Wing insignia, white on camouflage on upper surfaces, black on grey under surfaces.

MC 205 Veltro of the 1st Gruppo Caccia, RSI, sporting the "Asso di Bastoni" insignia on the engine cowl. Less than thirty Veltros operated alongside the Luftwaffe in the RSI after the Italian capitulation of September 1943.

Messerschmitt Bf 109E–4
Bulgarian Air Force

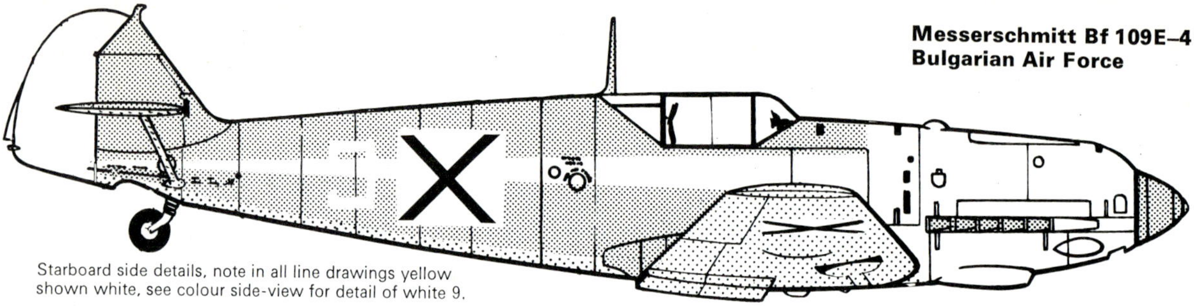

Starboard side details, note in all line drawings yellow shown white, see colour side-view for detail of white 9.

Span: 32ft. 4in. **Length:** 28ft. 4in. **Height:** 7ft. 6in.
Engine: Daimler Benz BD 601A 12-cylinder inverted liquid-cooled V of 1,100hp.
Armament: 2×20mm MG FF cannon plus 2×7.9mm machine guns.
Max. speed: 354 mph.
Weight: Empty 4,190lb. Loaded 5,875lb.

Pale Blue Grey

Pale Grey

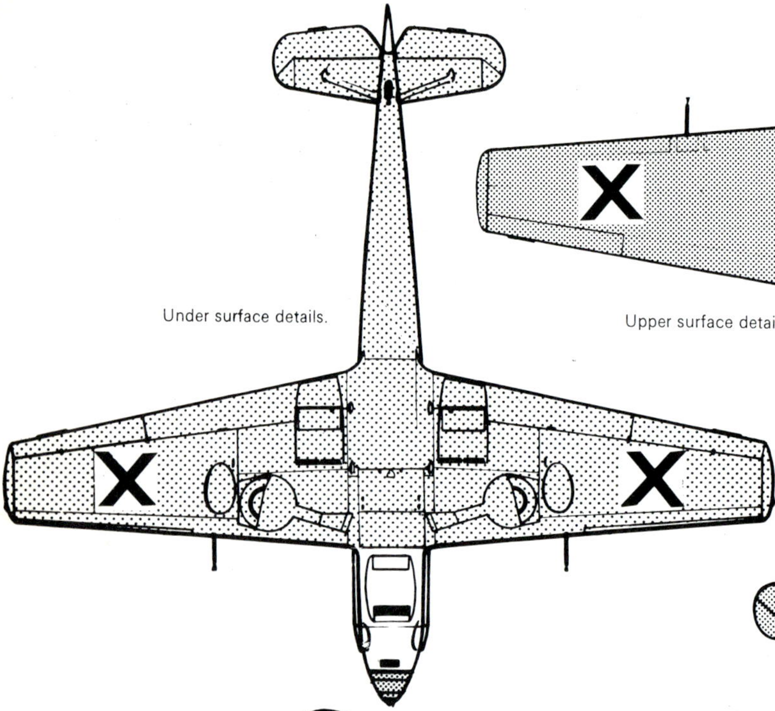

Under surface details.

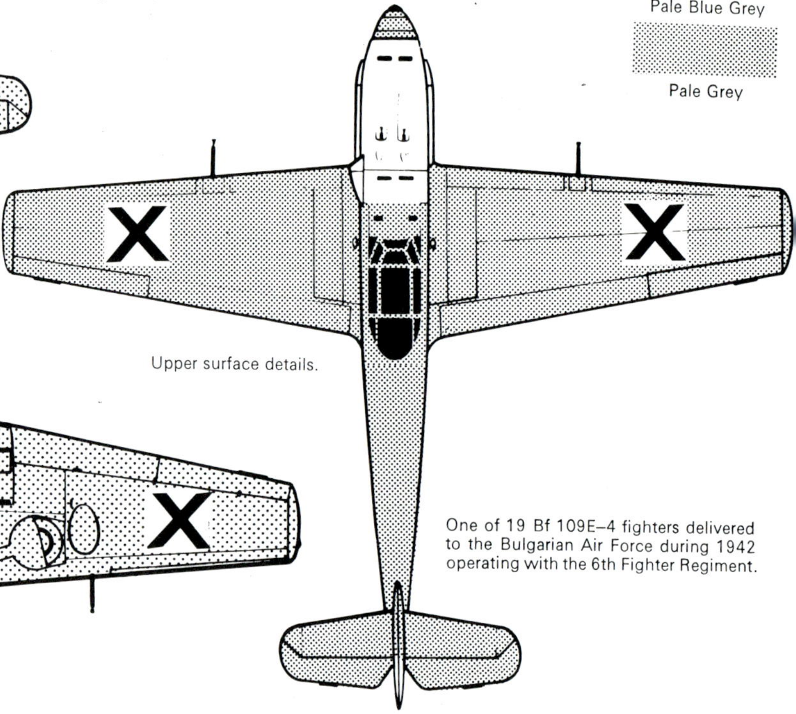

Upper surface details.

One of 19 Bf 109E–4 fighters delivered to the Bulgarian Air Force during 1942 operating with the 6th Fighter Regiment.

Green

White

Red

Dark Green

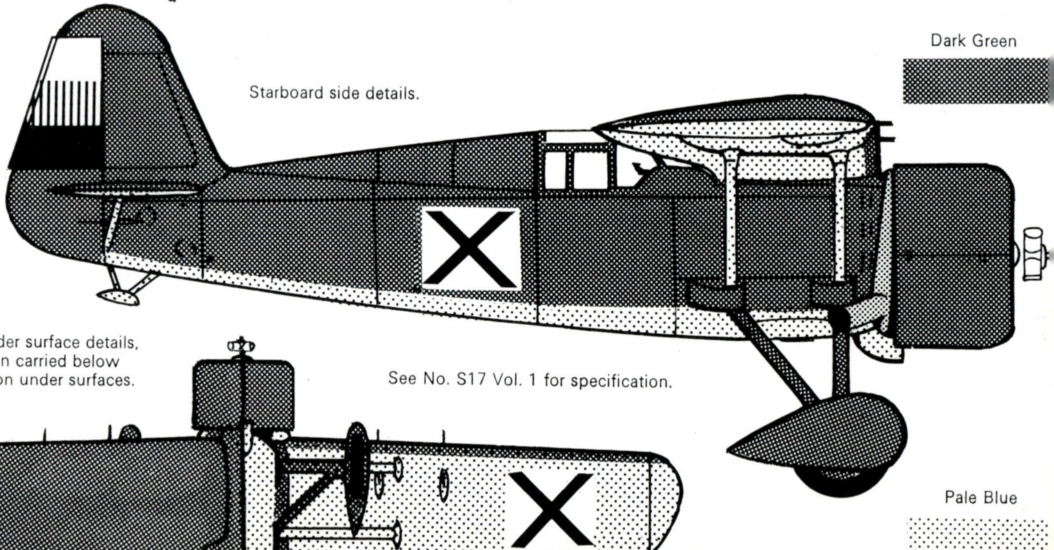

Starboard side details.

Upper and under surface details, note dark green carried below leading edge on under surfaces.

See No. S17 Vol. 1 for specification.

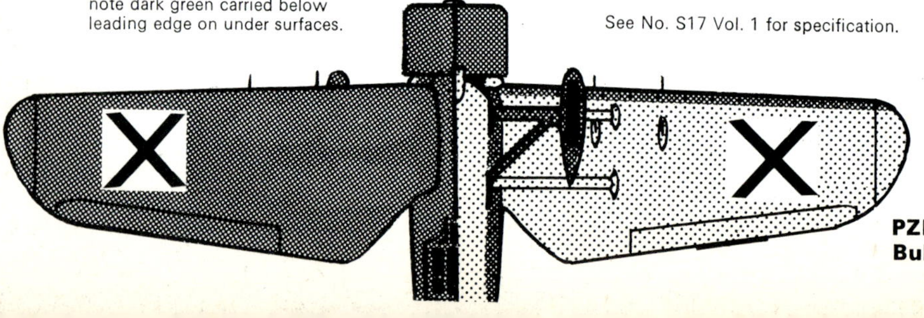

Pale Blue

PZL P–24E
Bulgarian Air Force

Messerschmitt Bf 109G–6
Regia Aeronautica

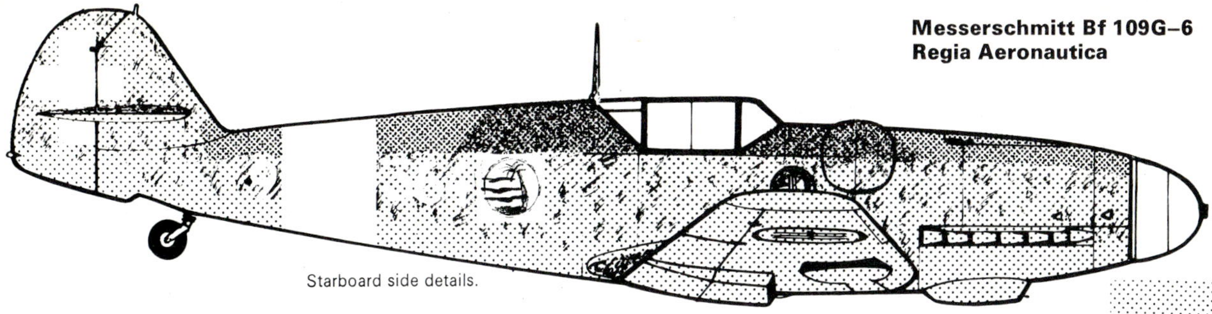

Starboard side details.

Span: 32ft. 6in. **Length:** 29ft. 8in. **Height:** 8ft. 6in.
Engine: Daimler Benz DB 605A 12-cylinder inverted liquid-cooled V of 1,475hp.
Armament: 2×13mm MG 131 machine guns and one engine mounted 20mm MG 151 cannon.
Max. speed: 385 mph.
Weight: Empty 5,900lb. Loaded 6,954lb.

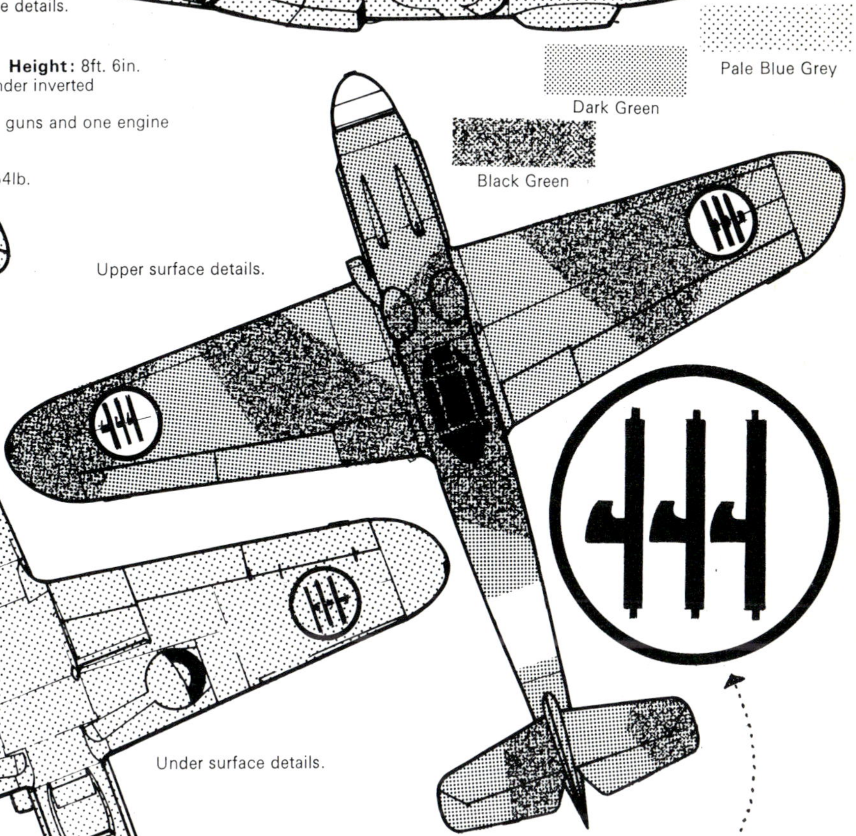

Upper surface details.

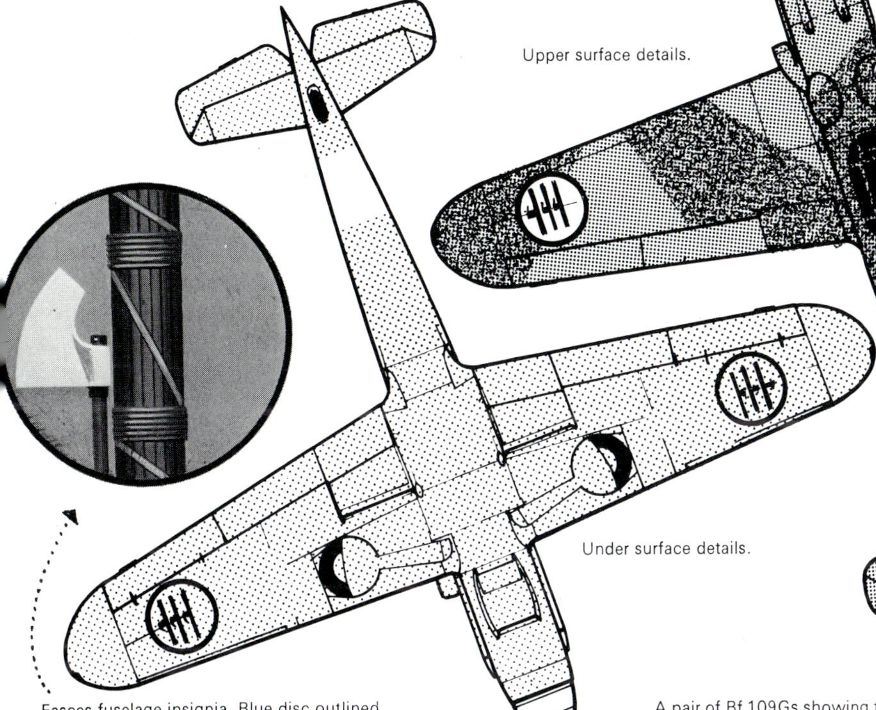

Under surface details.

Fasces wing insignia. Black on white on upper surfaces, black on grey under surfaces.

Fasces fuselage insignia. Blue disc outlined black with light to dark brown shaded faggots, silver axe blade, brown shaft, black lining.

A pair of Bf 109Gs showing the insignia of the 150 Gruppo, 53 Stormo on an Italian airfield sometime during 1943. Note the Coat of Arms of the House of Savoia is absent from the rudder white cross. (via G. Apostolo)

Mitsubishi A5M4
Japanese Naval Air Service

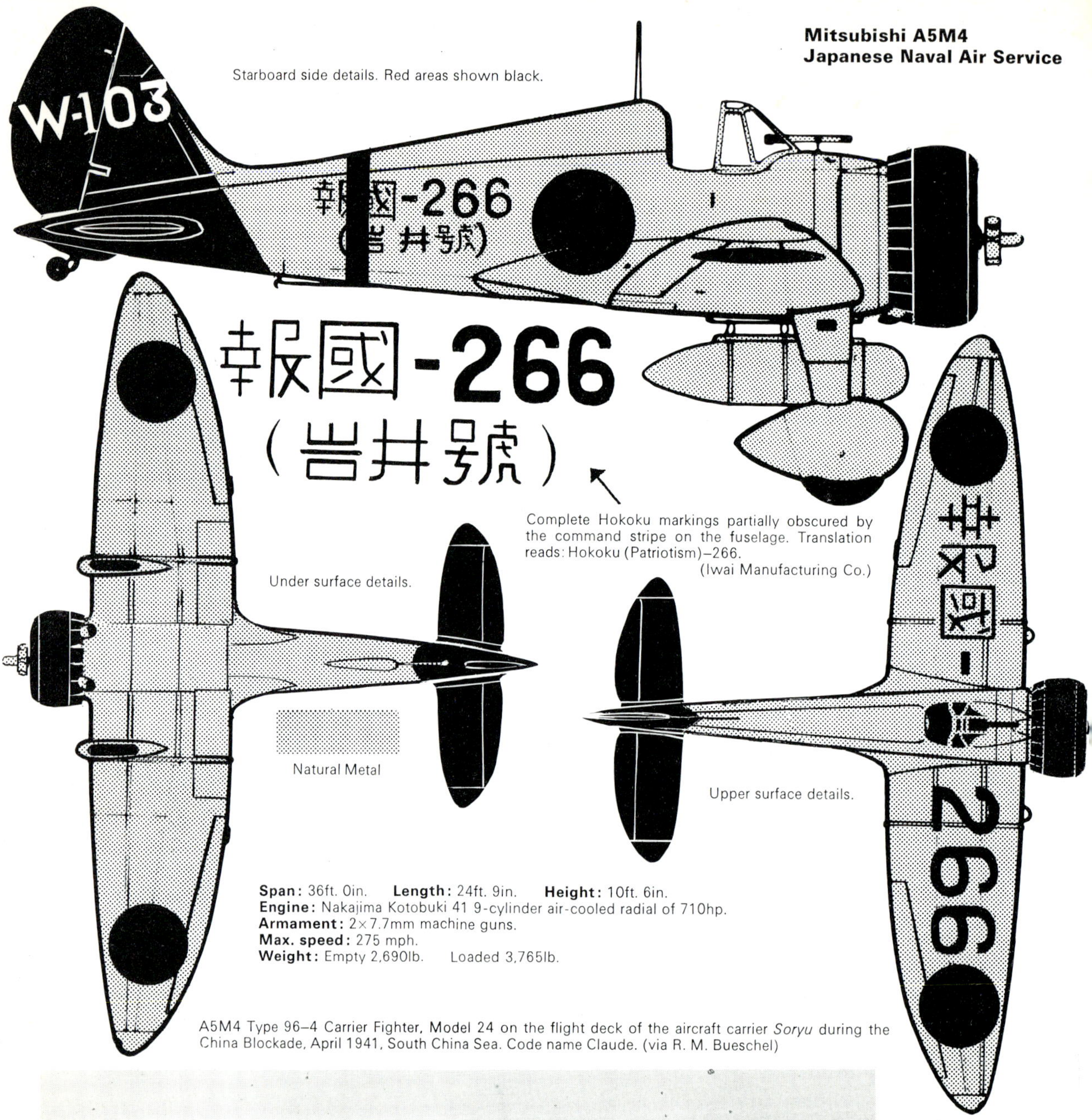

Span: 36ft. 0in. **Length:** 24ft. 9in. **Height:** 10ft. 6in.
Engine: Nakajima Kotobuki 41 9-cylinder air-cooled radial of 710hp.
Armament: 2×7.7mm machine guns.
Max. speed: 275 mph.
Weight: Empty 2,690lb. Loaded 3,765lb.

A5M4 Type 96–4 Carrier Fighter, Model 24 on the flight deck of the aircraft carrier *Soryu* during the China Blockade, April 1941, South China Sea. Code name Claude. (via R. M. Bueschel)

Nakajima Ki.27b
Manchoukuo Air Force

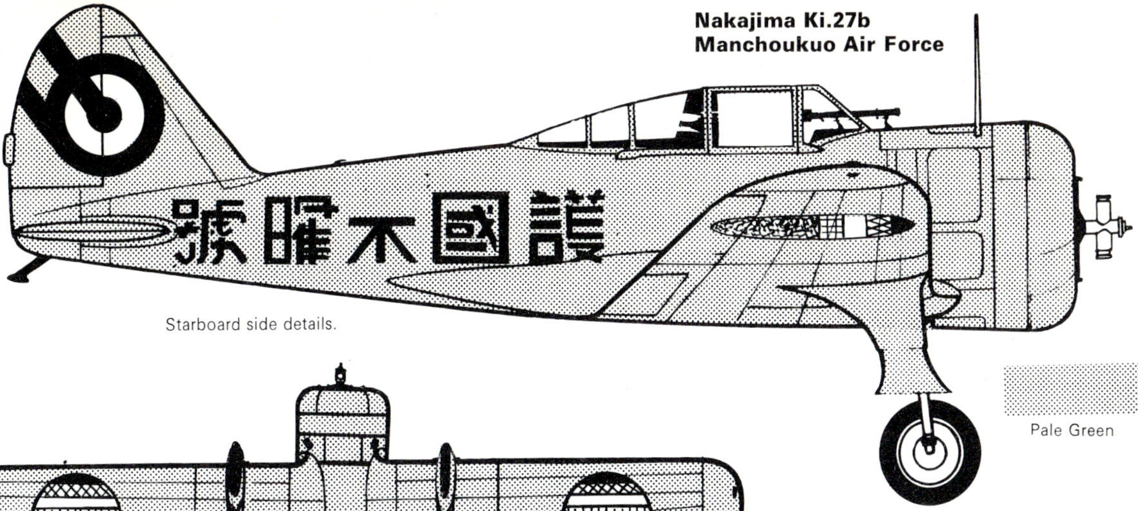

Starboard side details.

Pale Green

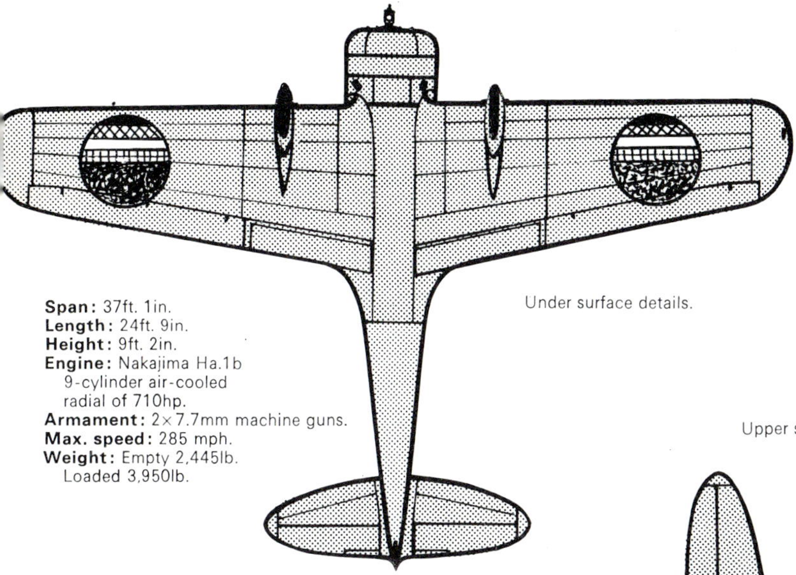

Under surface details.

Span: 37ft. 1in.
Length: 24ft. 9in.
Height: 9ft. 2in.
Engine: Nakajima Ha.1b 9-cylinder air-cooled radial of 710hp.
Armament: 2×7.7mm machine guns.
Max. speed: 285 mph.
Weight: Empty 2,445lb. Loaded 3,950lb.

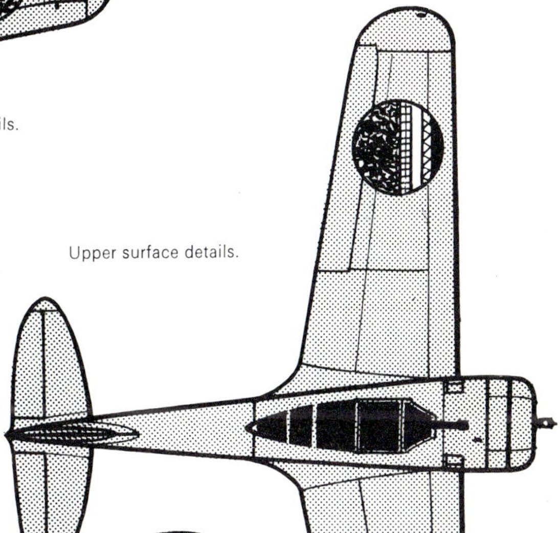

Upper surface details.

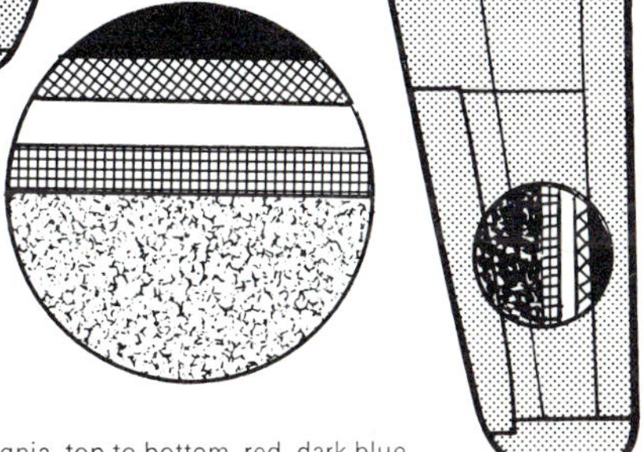

Manchoukuo insignia, top to bottom, red, dark blue, white, dark brown, yellow.

Ki.27b still in use as a fighter trainer by the Manchoukuoan Air Force as late as 1944, this photo shows the aircraft illustrated in colour. (Asahigraph via R. M. Bueschel)

Line-up of new Manchoukuo Ki.27b fighters in September 1942. Code name Nate. (Hiko-Nippon via R. M. Bueschel)

Nakajima Ki.84a Hayate
Japanese Army Air Force

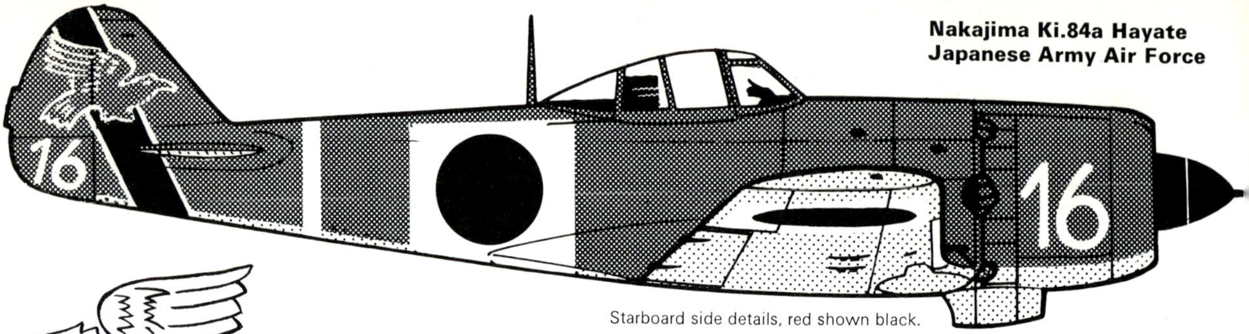

Starboard side details, red shown black.

Detail of eagle on fin and rudder.

Last of a long line of Nakajima fighters to go into production for the JAAF, the Ki.84 introduced into service during the summer of 1944 remained a thorn in the side of the Allies until the Japanese surrender.

Upper surface details.

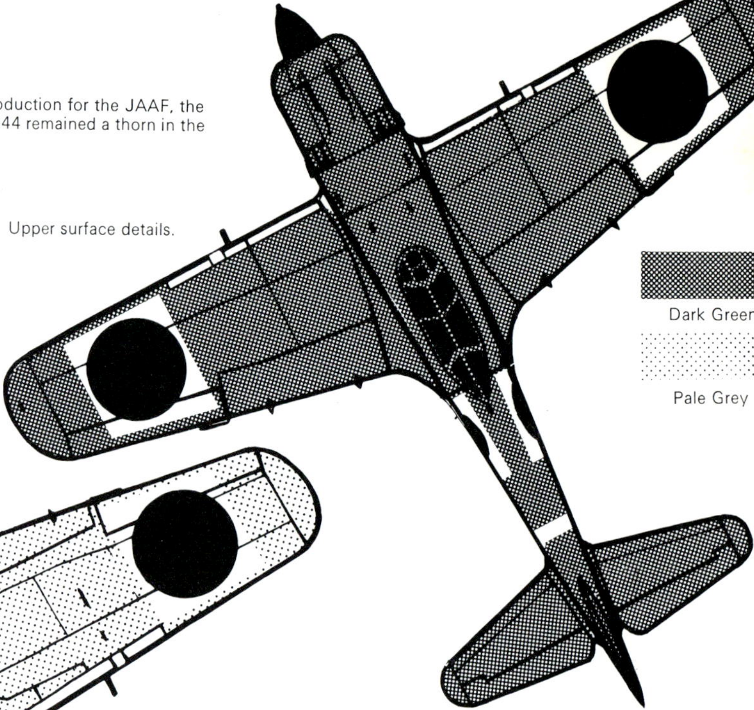

Dark Green

Pale Grey

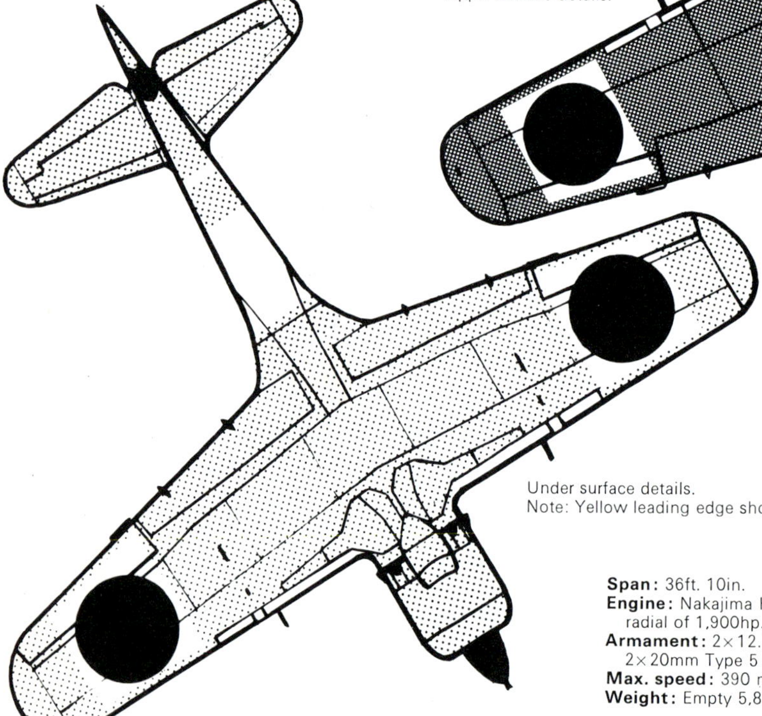

Under surface details.
Note: Yellow leading edge shown white.

Span: 36ft. 10in. **Length:** 32ft. 6in. **Height:** 11ft. 1in.
Engine: Nakajima Ha.45/11 Type 4 18-cylinder air-cooled radial of 1,900hp.
Armament: 2×12.7mm Type 103 machine guns plus 2×20mm Type 5 cannon.
Max. speed: 390 mph.
Weight: Empty 5,865lb. Loaded 9,195lb.

Ki.84a of the 520th Temporary Interception Regiment, Home Island Defence, Nakatsu airfield, March–May 1945. The diagonal tail stripe is medium blue edged with white, the spinner is also blue. Crudely applied 33 in white, otherwise as 16 above.

Medium Blue

A

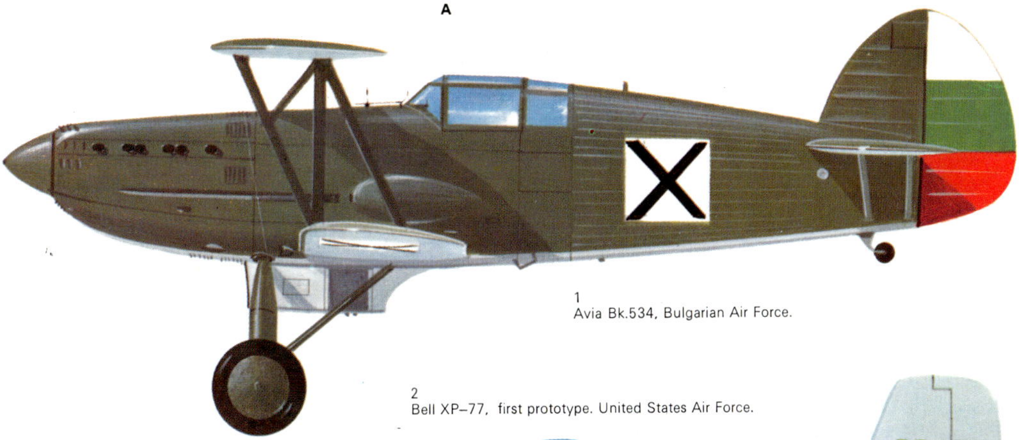

1
Avia Bk.534, Bulgarian Air Force.

2
Bell XP–77, first prototype. United States Air Force.

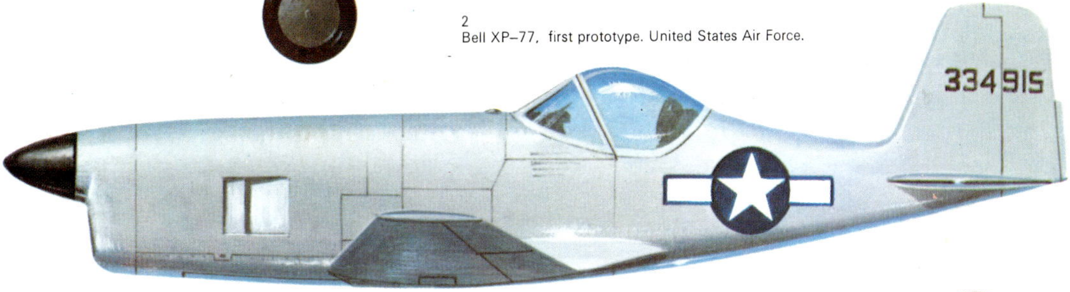

3
Curtiss Mohawk Mk.IV, No. 25 Fighter Leader School, RAF.

4
Curtiss YP–37, USAAF.

5
Curtiss P–40C Tomahawk, 23rd Fighter Group,
ex-American Volunteer Group, USAAF, Kunming, China, 1942.

B

1
Curtiss XP–46, USAAF.

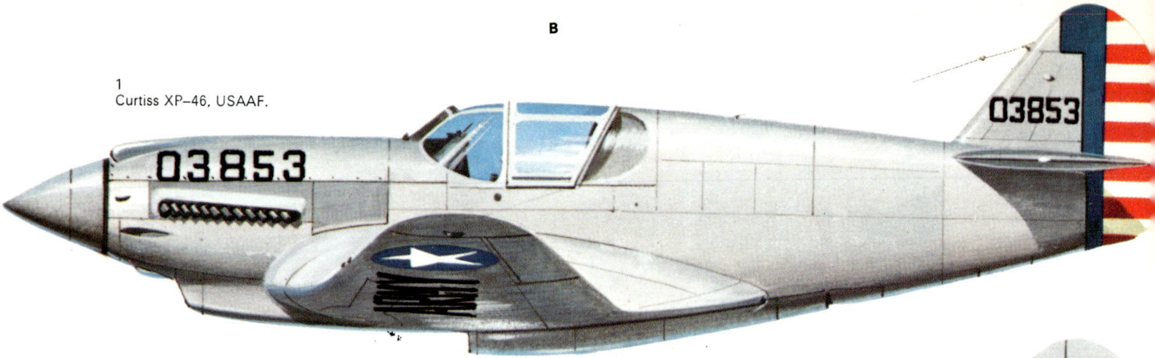

2
Curtiss XP–40Q Warhawk, second prototype, USAAF.

3
Curtiss XP–60C, USAAF.

4
Curtiss YP–60E, last of the XP–60 series of prototypes, USAAF.

5
Focke-Wulf Fw 190F–8, Gruppenadjutant 2./SG 2 "Immelmann", Hungary, winter 1944–1945.

© WARRD–

C

1
General Motors (Fisher) XP–75 Eagle, USAAF.

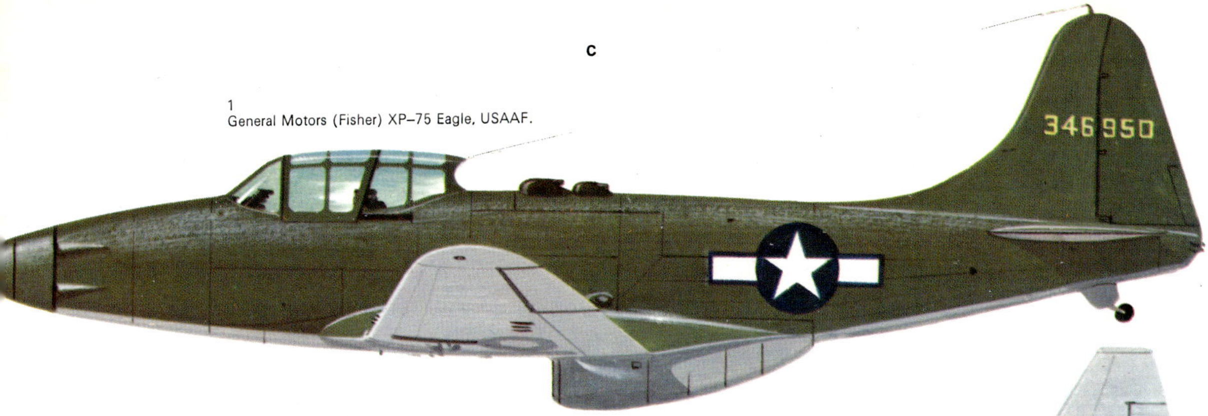

2
General Motors (Fisher) P–57 Eagle, USAAF.

3
Grumman XF5F–1, US Navy.

4
Hawker Typhoon Ib, No. 440 Squadron, 2nd Tactical Air Force, RAF, Royal Canadian Air Force. 1944–1945.

5
Hawker Tempest V, No. 80 Squadron, 2nd Tactical Air Force, RAF. 1944–1945.

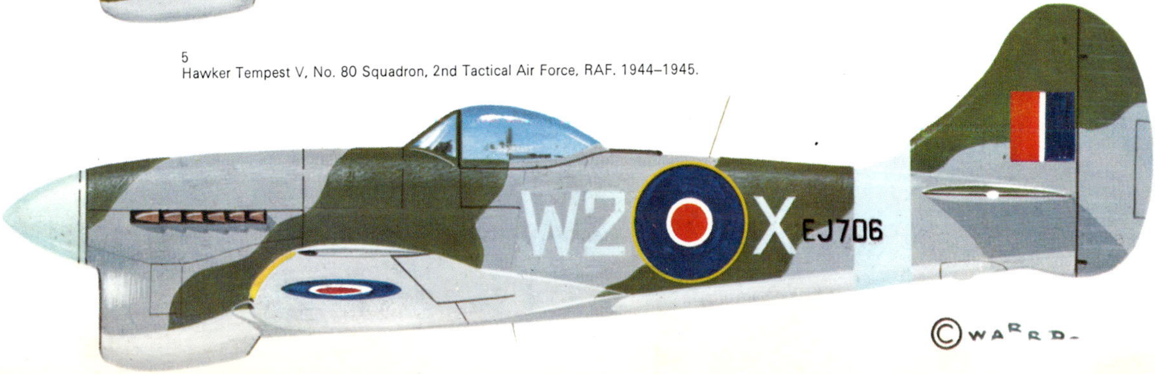

D

1
Industria Aeronautica Romana IAR 81,
Two-seat fighter trainer, Royal Rumanian Air Force.

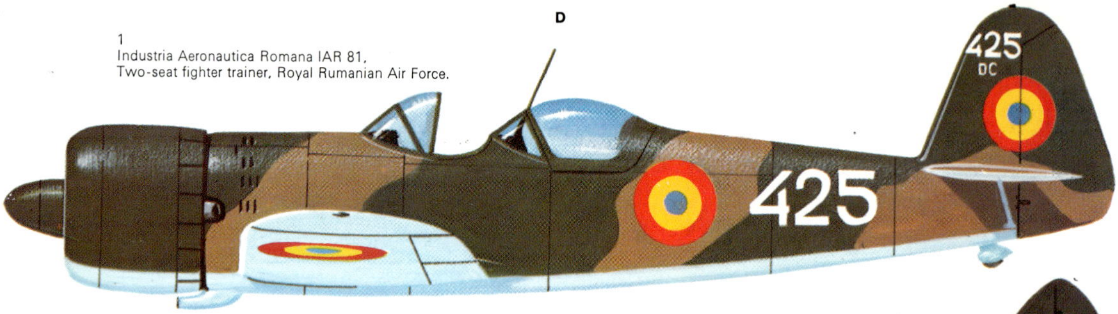

2
I–17, Russian Air Force.

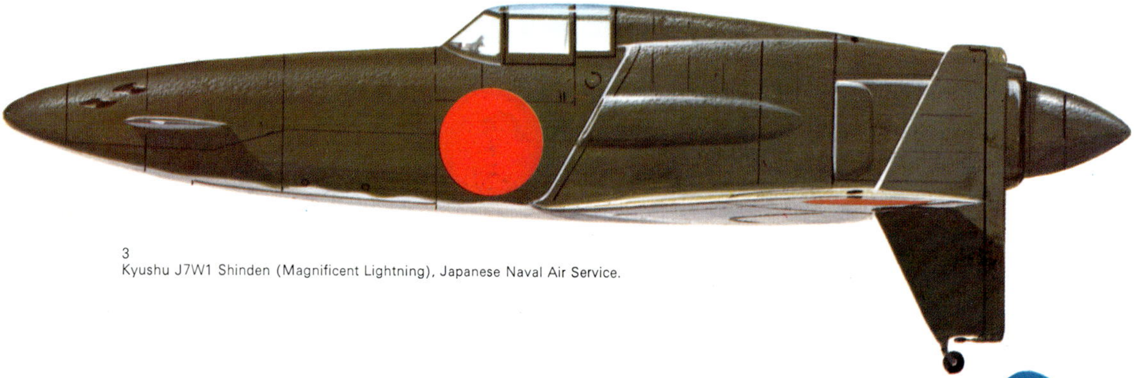

3
Kyushu J7W1 Shinden (Magnificent Lightning), Japanese Naval Air Service.

4
Lavochkin La.7. Flown by Lt.-Col. Ivan Kojedub, winter 1944–1945.

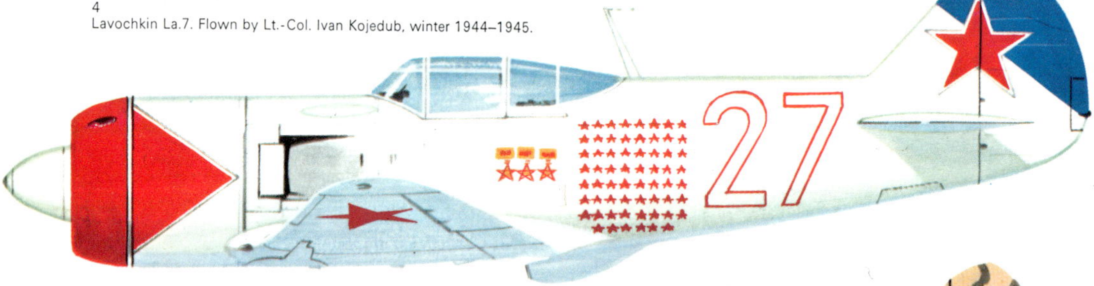

5
Macchi MC 205 Veltro (Greyhound),
1 Gruppo, Aviazione della RSI, Italy 1943.

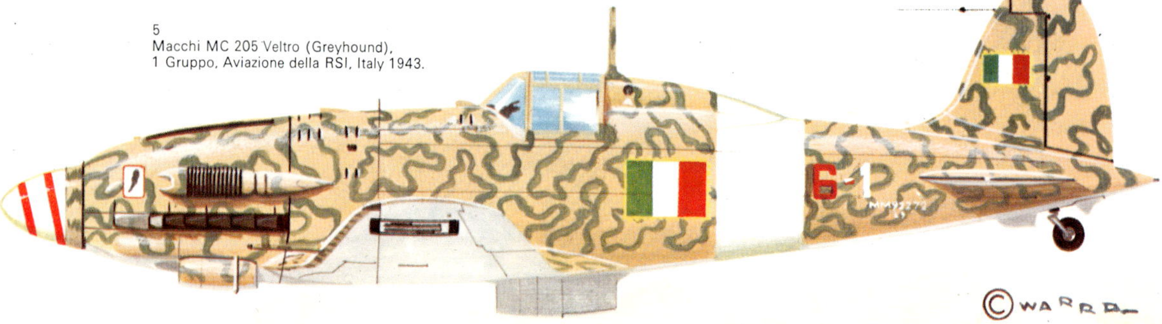

©WARR

E

1
Messerschmitt Bf 109E–4, 6th Fighter Regiment, Bulgarian Air Force, 1942.

2
Messerschmitt Bf 109G–6, 150 Gruppo, 53 Stormo, Regia Aeronautica, Italy 1943.

3
Mitsubishi A5M4, Carrier *Soryu*, China Blockade, 1943. South China Sea, April 1941.

4
Nakajima Ki.27b–Kai, Manchoukuo Air Force, 1944.

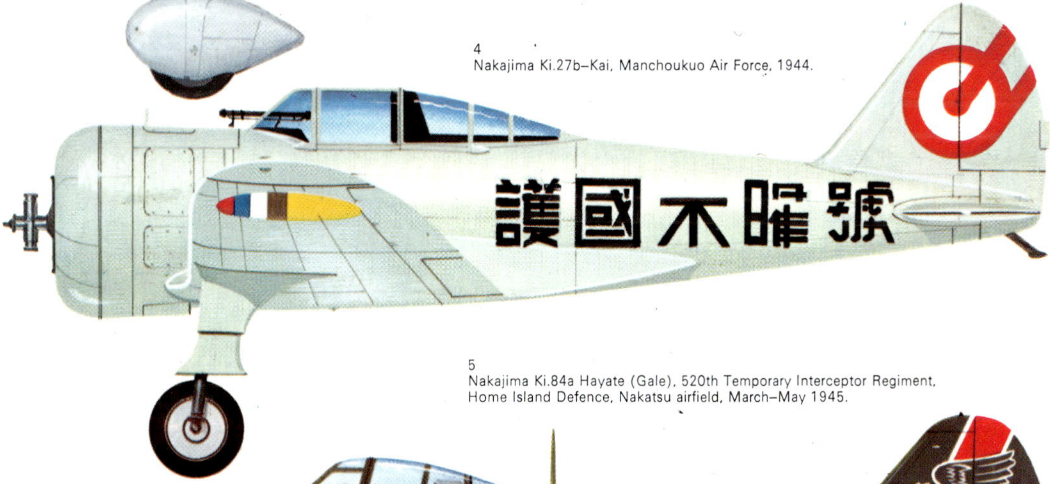

5
Nakajima Ki.84a Hayate (Gale), 520th Temporary Interceptor Regiment, Home Island Defence, Nakatsu airfield, March–May 1945.

F

1
North American P–51 Mustang modified for low-level photo reconnaissance with camera mounted in rear cockpit in experimental scheme, USAAF.

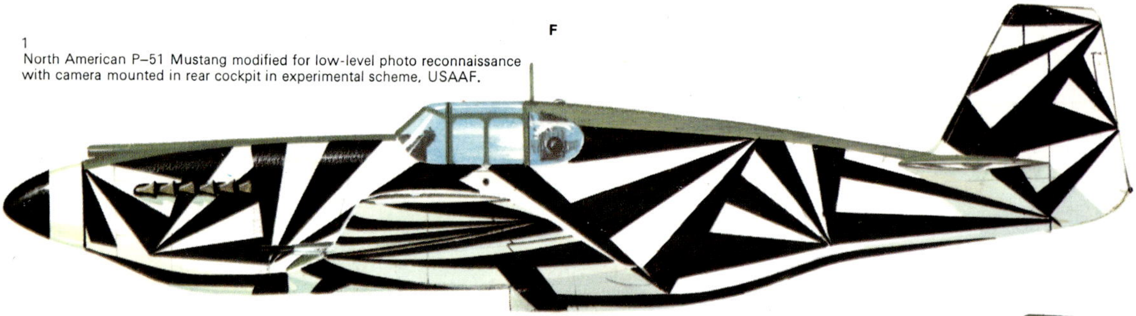

2
North American Mustang IA, No. 35 Photographic Reconnaissance Wing, 2nd TAF, RAF. Summer 1944.

3
North American Mustang III, No. 122 "Bombay" Squadron, No. 122 Wing, 2nd TAF, RAF. June 1944.

4
North American P–51B Mustang, Swiss Air Force, 1945.

5
North American P–51D Mustang, AURI, 1970.

G

1
Reggiane Re.2001, Regia Aeronautica. Experimental installation of liquid air bomb, Furbara Firing Range, Italy, March 1943.

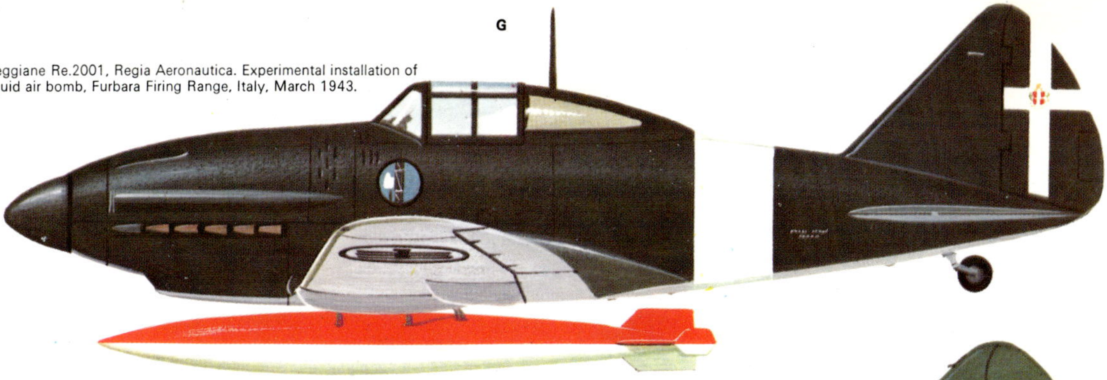

2
Republic P–43 Lancer, 1st Pursuit Group, 1941 War Games.

3
Republic P–47D Thunderbolt, 58th Fighter Group, 310th Fighter Squadron, 5th Air Force, SWPA. Saidor, New Guinea, 1943.

4
Republic P–47D Thunderbolt, 1st Air Commando Group, 10th Air Force, CBI. Burma/India 1944–1945.

5
Republic P–47D Thunderbolt, Chilean Air Force.

H

1
Northrop XP–56, first prototype. USAAF.

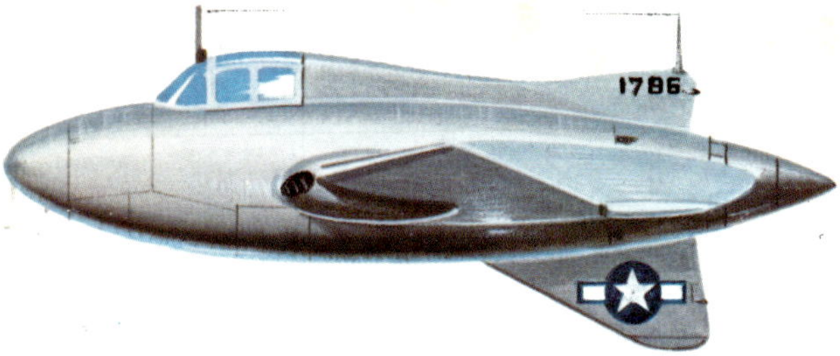

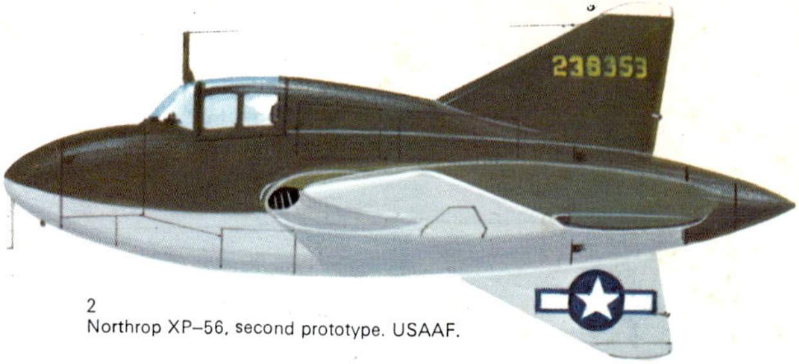

2
Northrop XP–56, second prototype. USAAF.

3
Vickers Supermarine Spitfire Mk.IX, No. 403 Squadron, Royal Canadian Air Force, 2nd TAF, RAF. February 1944.

4
Vickers Supermarine Spitfire Mk.IX, GC II/5, French Air Force, Hanoi, French Indo-China, 1946–1947.

5
Vultee XP–54, USAAF.

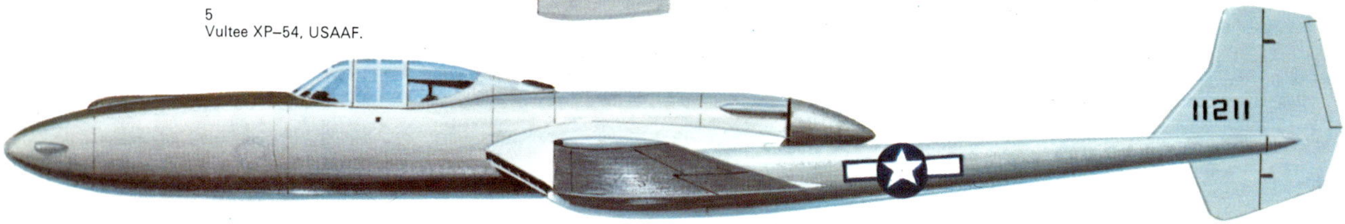

6
Valtion Lentokonetehdas V. L. Myrsky, Finnish Air Force. Prior 1 April 1945.

7
Valtion Lentokonetehdas V. L. Myrsky II, Finnish Air Force. Post 1 April 1945

©WARD

North American Mustang Ia
2nd TAF, Royal Air Force

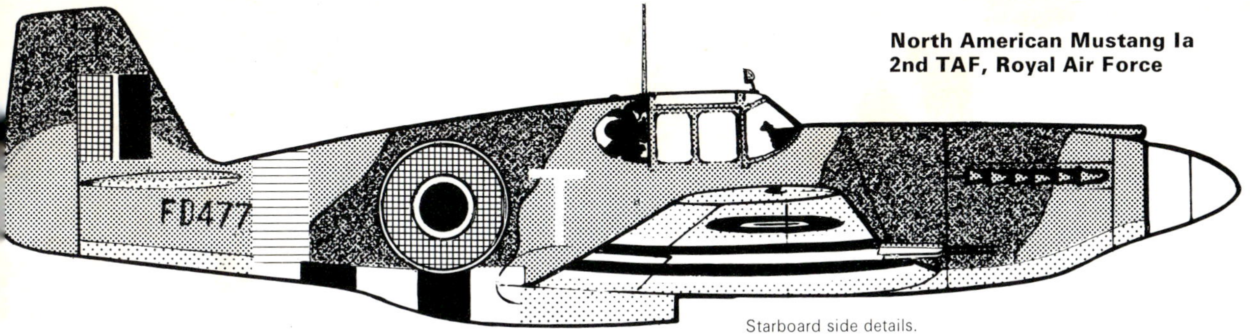

Starboard side details.

Span: 37ft. 0in. **Length:** 32ft. 3in. **Height:** 12ft. 2in.
Engine: Allison V–1710–39 12-cylinder liquid-cooled V of 1,150hp.
Armament: 4× 20mm cannon.
Max. speed: 387 mph.
Weight: Empty 6,550lb. Loaded 8,800lb.

Equivalent to the USAAF P–51/F–6A.

Sky

Medium Grey

Dark Green

Pale Grey

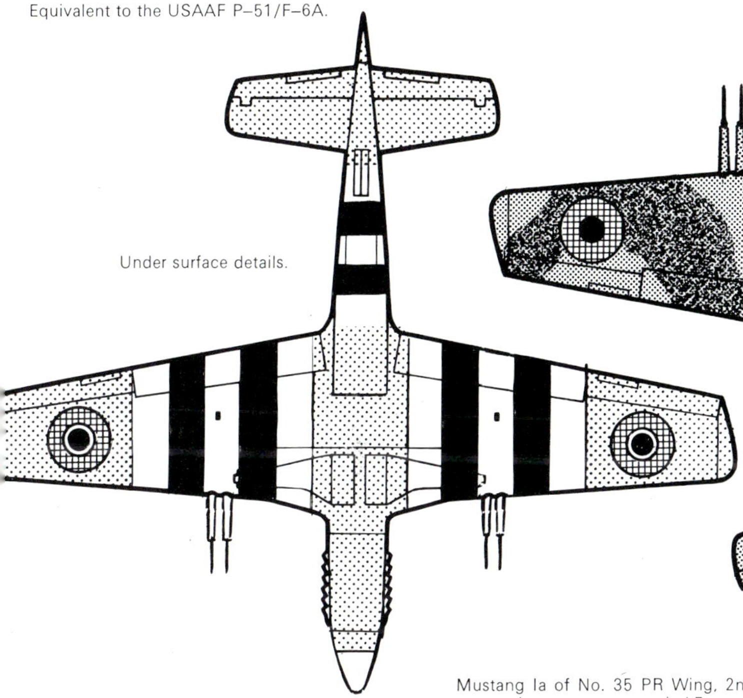

Under surface details.

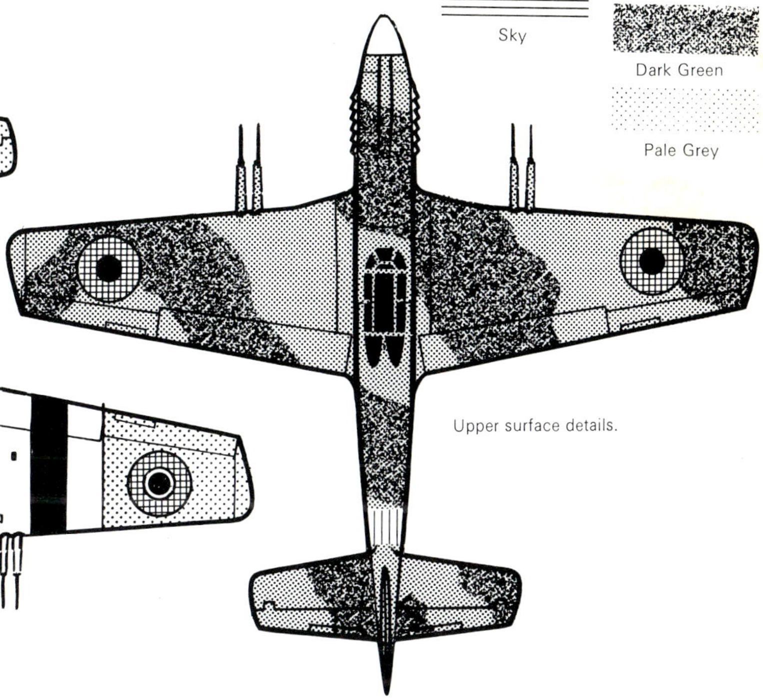

Upper surface details.

Mustang Ia of No. 35 PR Wing, 2nd TAF revving-up prior to take-off on a low-level armed reconnaissance over occupied Europe, summer 1944.

North American P–51 Mustang USAAF

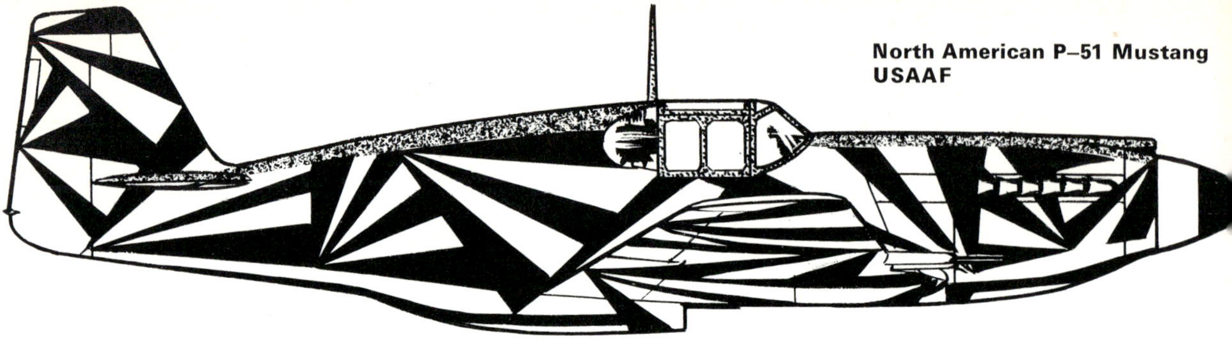

Starboard side details.

Specification as for Mustang Ia.

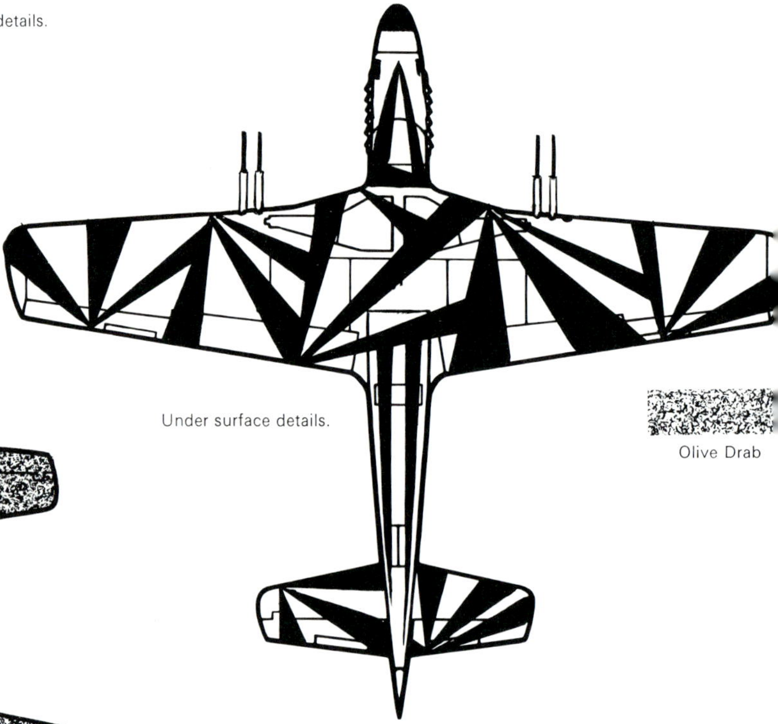

Under surface details.

Olive Drab

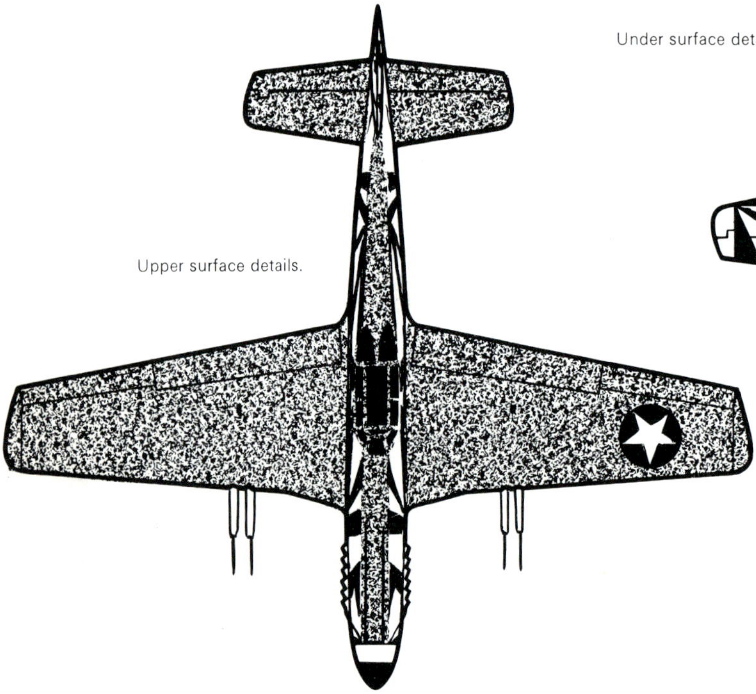

Upper surface details.

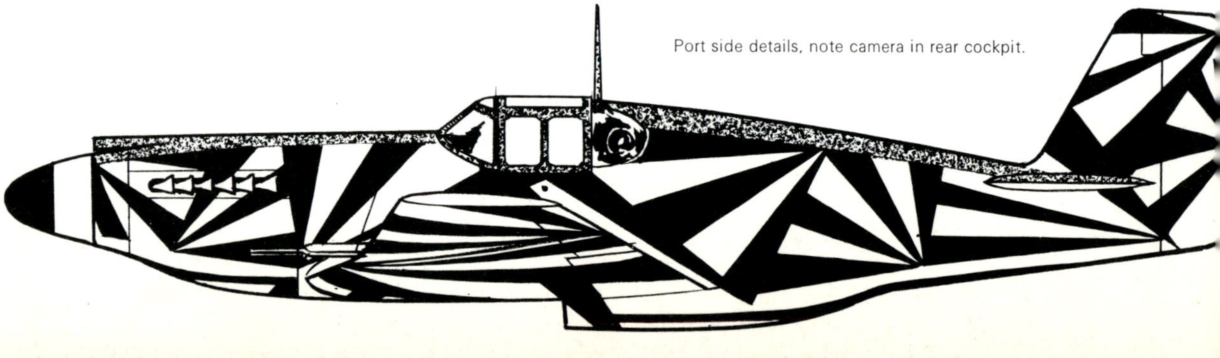

Port side details, note camera in rear cockpit.

Certainly the most bizarre splinter camouflage scheme to appear in World War II, was the black and white scheme on this P–51 modified for low-level armed reconnaissance role with an oblique camera in the rear cockpit, clearly seen in the bottom photograph. (USAF)

North American Mustang III 2nd TAF, RAF

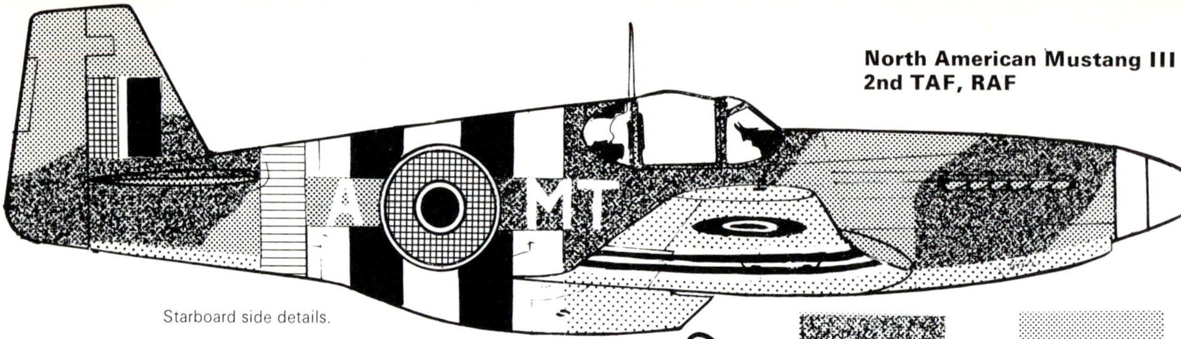

Starboard side details.

Span: 37ft. 0in. **Length:** 32ft. 3in. **Height:** 13ft. 8in.
Engine: Packard V–1650–3 12-cylinder liquid-cooled V of 1,595hp.
Armament: 4×.5in machine guns plus 2×1,000lb bombs.
Max. speed: 440 mph.
Weight: Empty 6,985lb. Loaded 11,800lb.

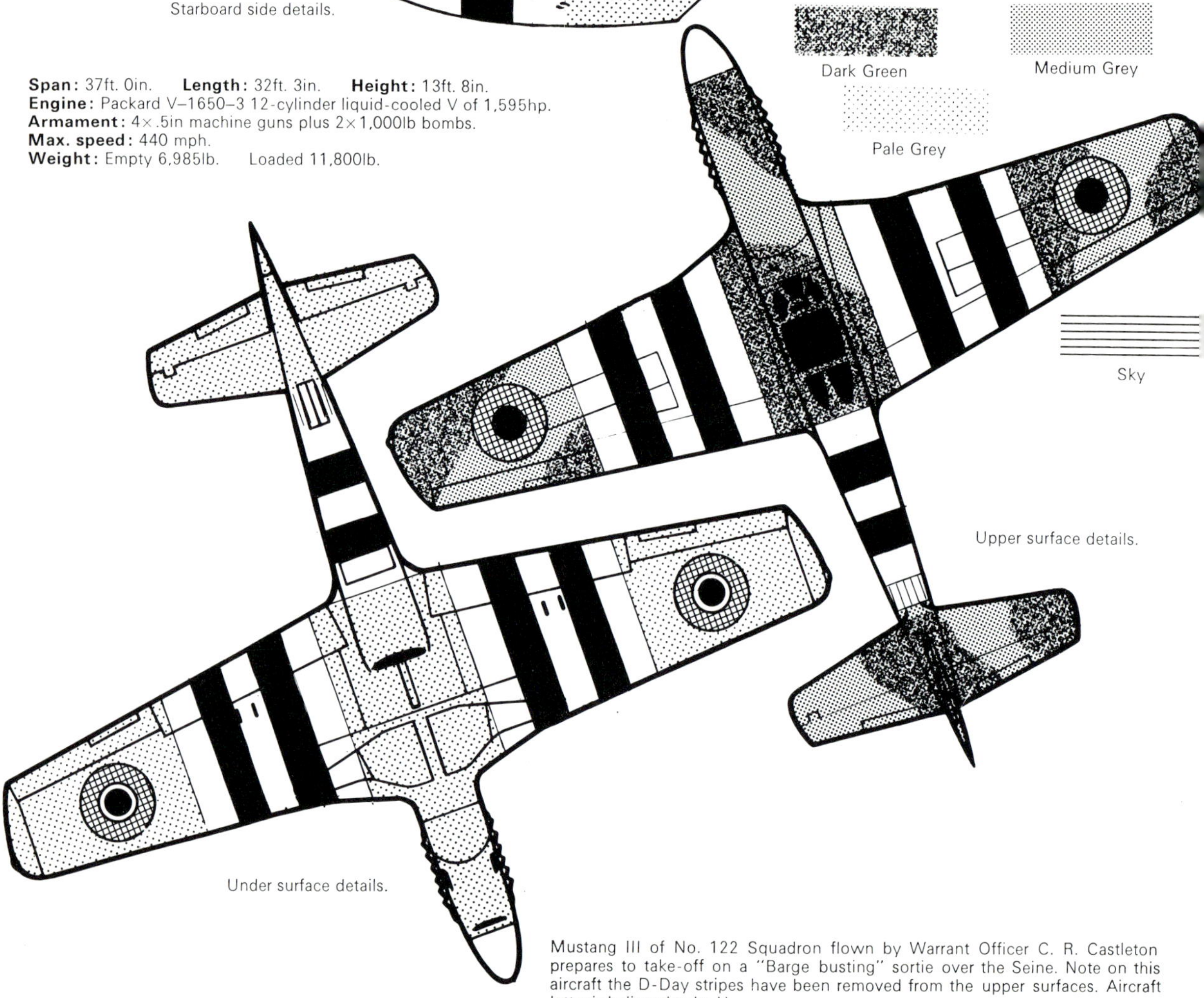

Upper surface details.

Under surface details.

Mustang III of No. 122 Squadron flown by Warrant Officer C. R. Castleton prepares to take-off on a "Barge busting" sortie over the Seine. Note on this aircraft the D-Day stripes have been removed from the upper surfaces. Aircraft letter is believed to be H.

North American P–51B Mustang
Swiss Air Force

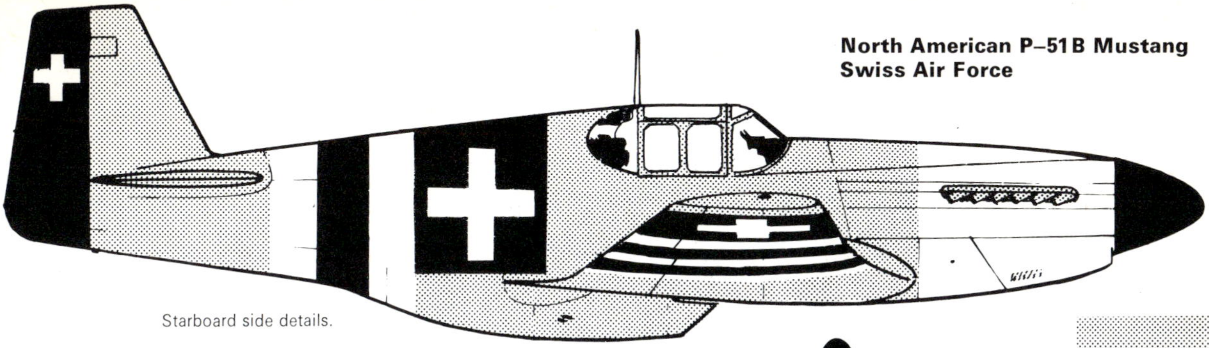

Starboard side details.

Natural Metal

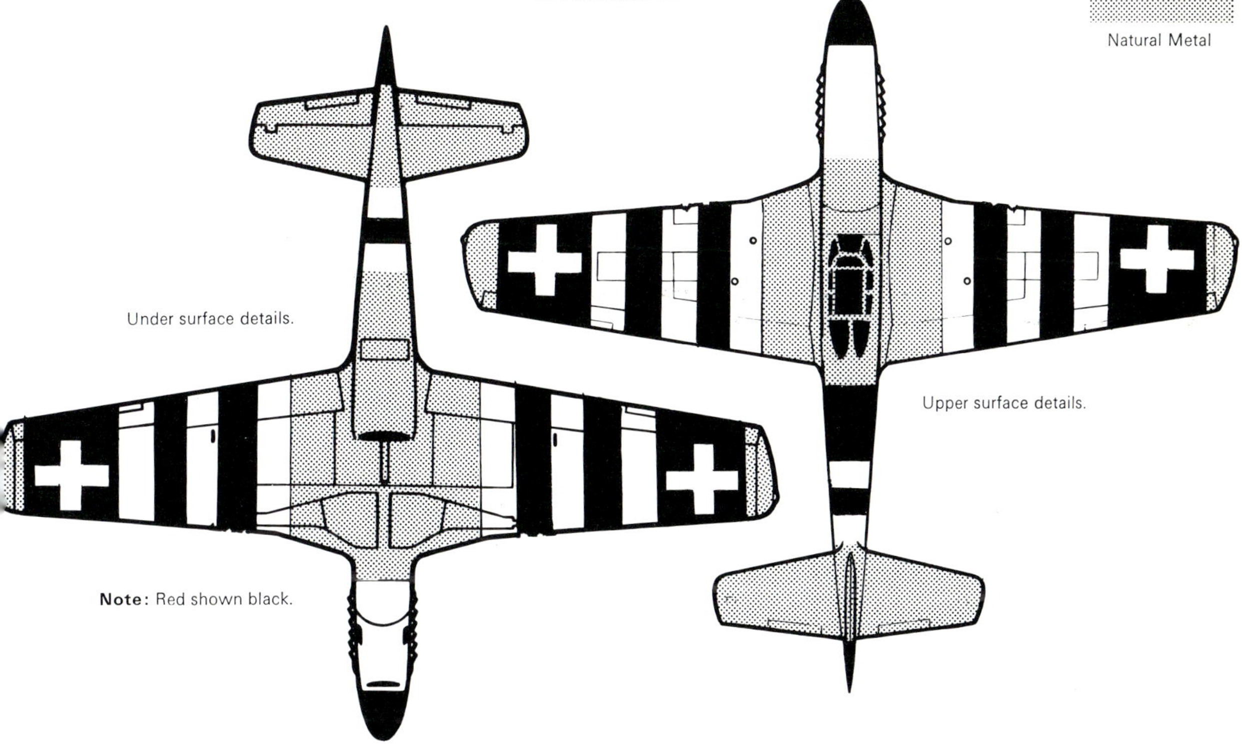

Under surface details.

Note: Red shown black.

Upper surface details.

A World War II USAAF 8th Air Force casualty which forced landed in Switzerland, repaired and test flown by the Swiss Air Force. No doubt the performance was an eye opener to the Swiss and resulted in the subsequent post-war re-equipment of their fighter force with the P–51D, an example of which is illustrated to the right and below, note the last three digits of the code repeated on the lower engine cowl.

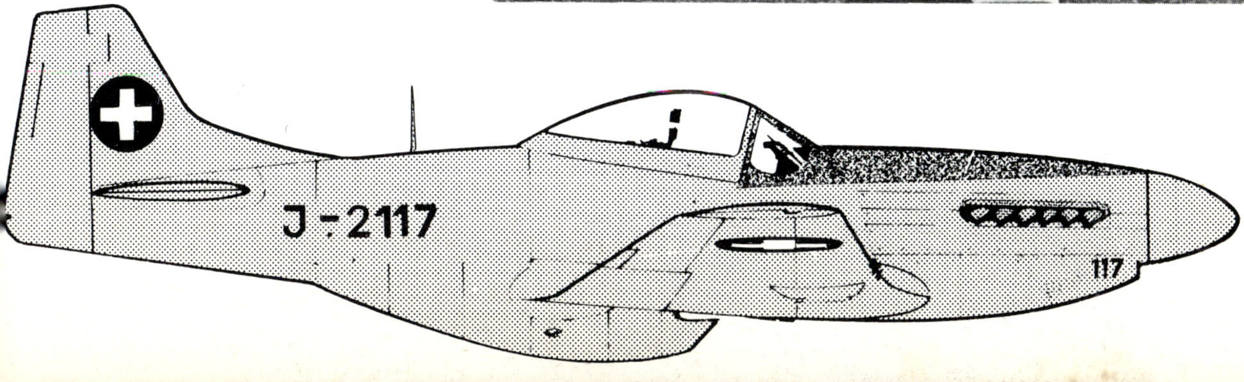

North American P–51D Mustang
AURI – Indonesian Air Force

Natural Metal

Starboard side details.

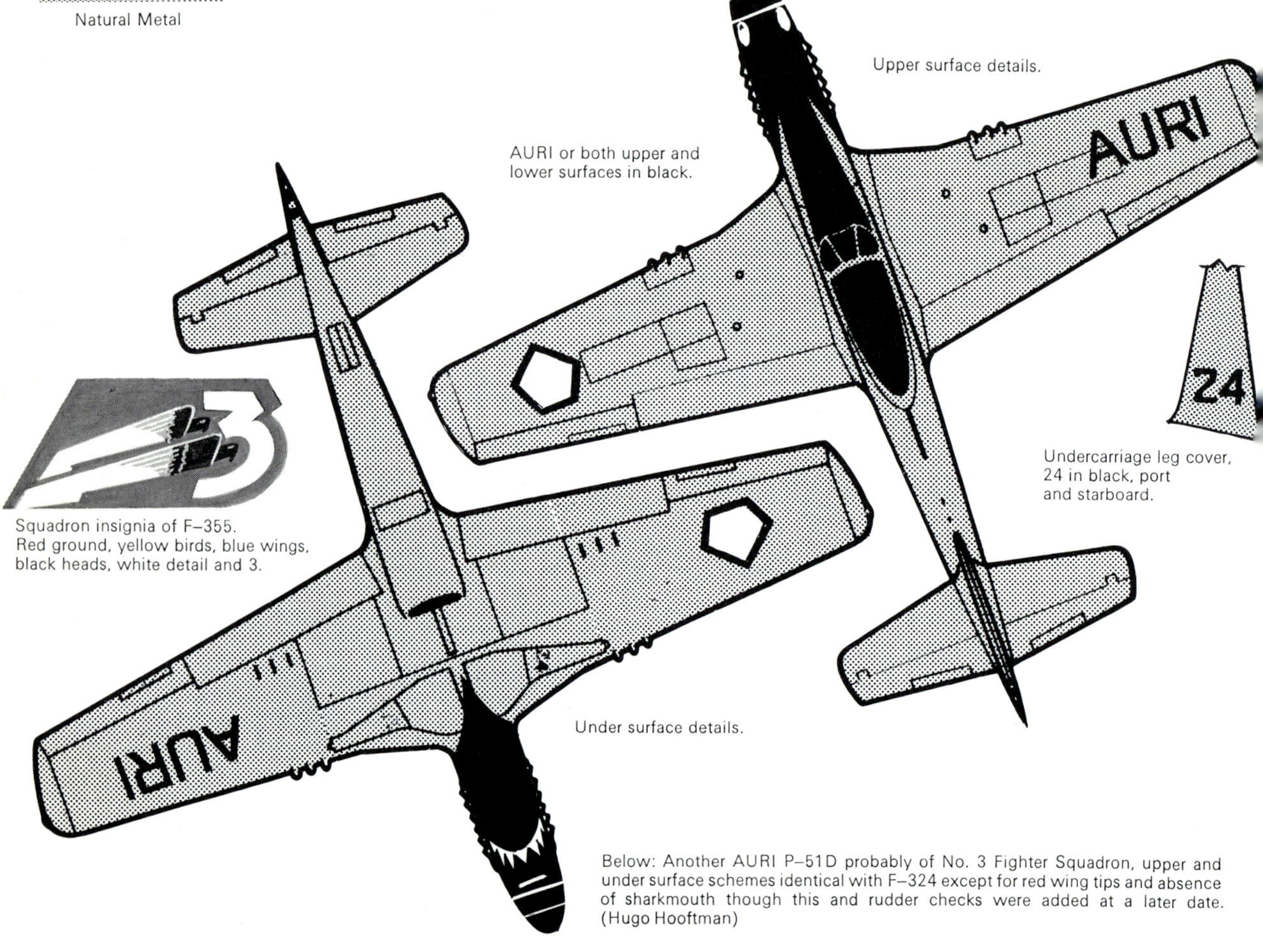

Upper surface details.

AURI or both upper and lower surfaces in black.

Squadron insignia of F–355. Red ground, yellow birds, blue wings, black heads, white detail and 3.

Undercarriage leg cover, 24 in black, port and starboard.

Under surface details.

Below: Another AURI P–51D probably of No. 3 Fighter Squadron, upper and under surface schemes identical with F–324 except for red wing tips and absence of sharkmouth though this and rudder checks were added at a later date. (Hugo Hooftman)

Rear view of the 1st prototype in overall natural metal finish. (Peter M. Bowers)

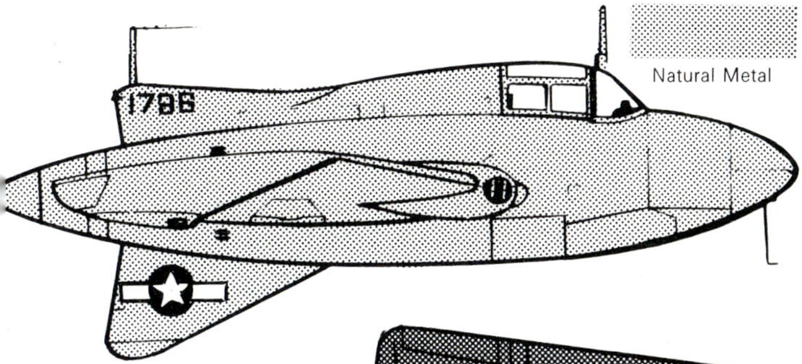

Starboard side details.

Span: 42ft. 5in. **Length:** 27ft. 6½in. **Height:** 13ft. 5½in.
Engine: Pratt and Whitney R–2800–29 18-cylinder air-cooled radial of 2,000hp.
Armament: 2×20mm cannon plus 4×.5in machine guns.
Max. speed: 460 mph estimated.
Weight: Empty 8,720lb. Loaded 12,135lb.

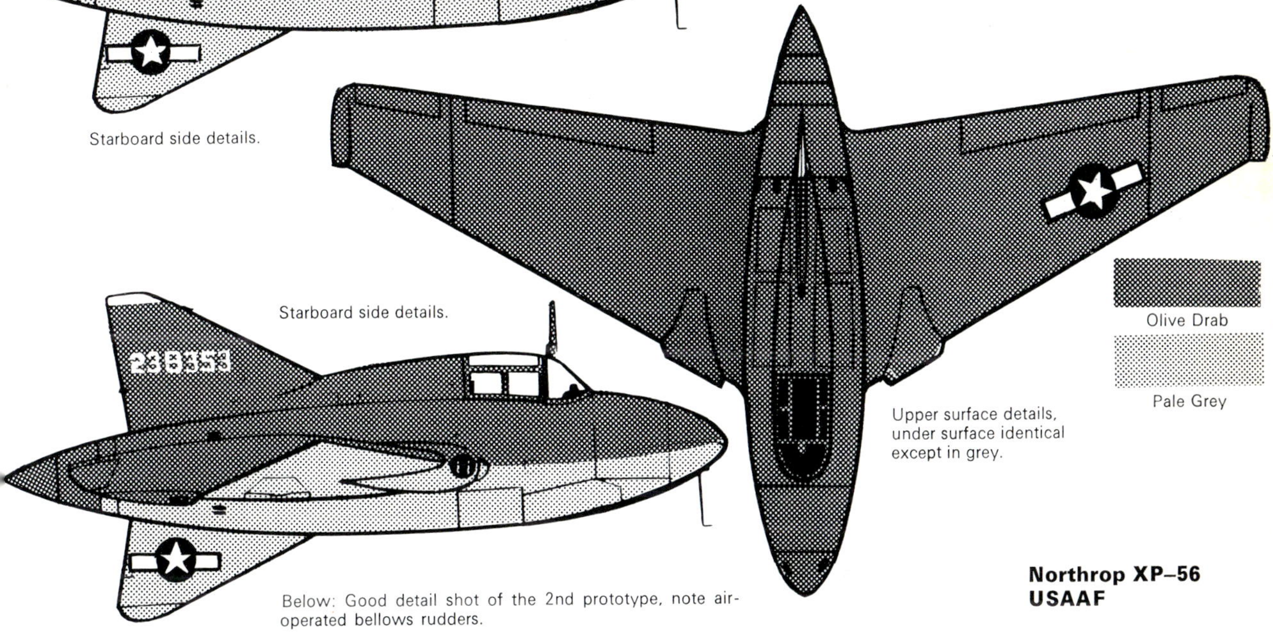

Upper surface details, under surface identical except in grey.

Starboard side details.

Northrop XP–56
USAAF

Below: Good detail shot of the 2nd prototype, note air-operated bellows rudders.

Republic P–43 Lancer
USAAF

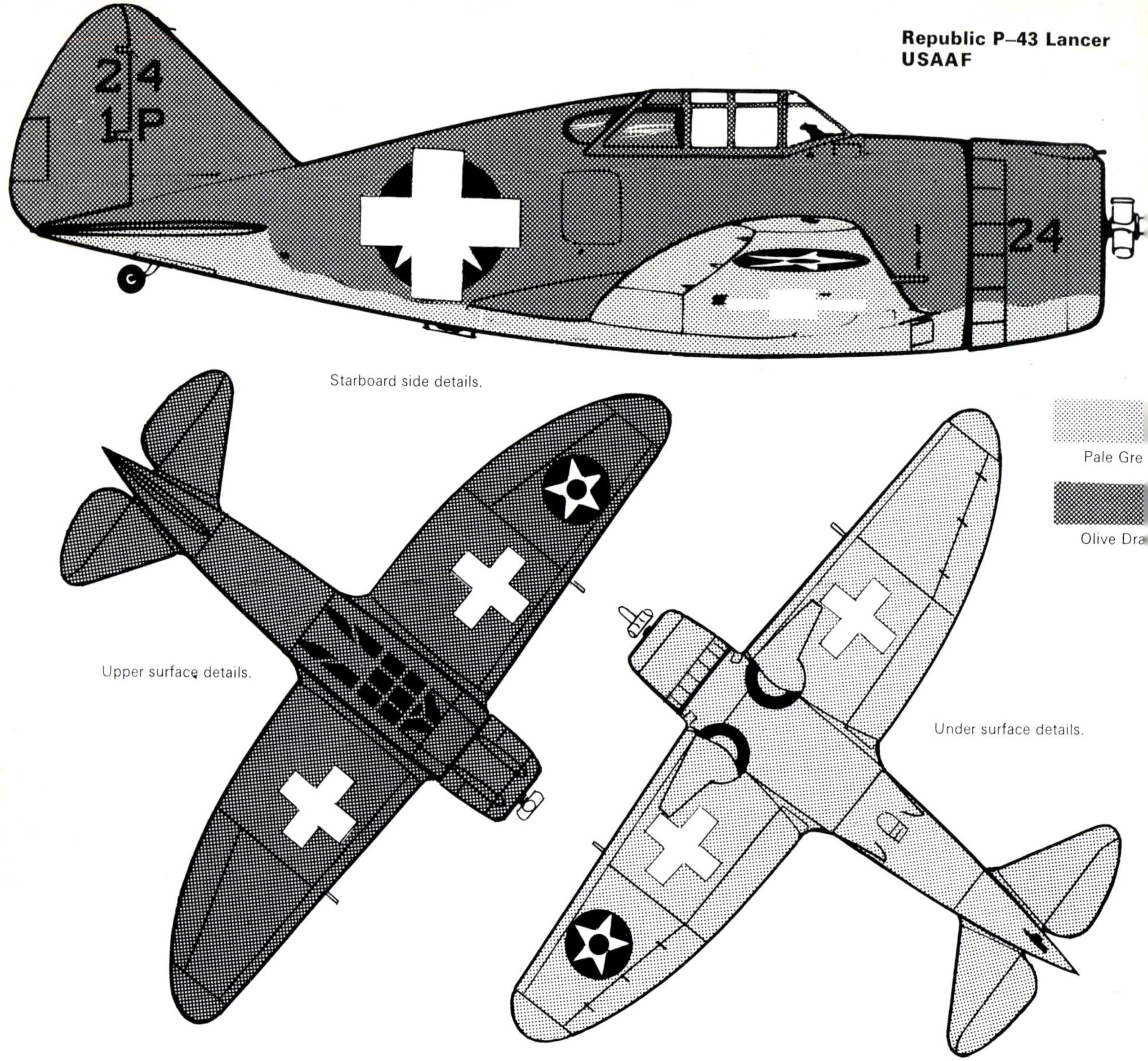

Starboard side details.

Upper surface details.

Under surface details.

Selection of views showing the white cross marking used by one of the opposing sides during the 1941 War Games, applied in a washable paint which quickly flaked off. Note the B–25 in the background similarly marked. (Fred C. Dickey Jr.)

Specification may be found in No. S17 Volume 1.

Republic P–47D Thunderbolt
USAAF

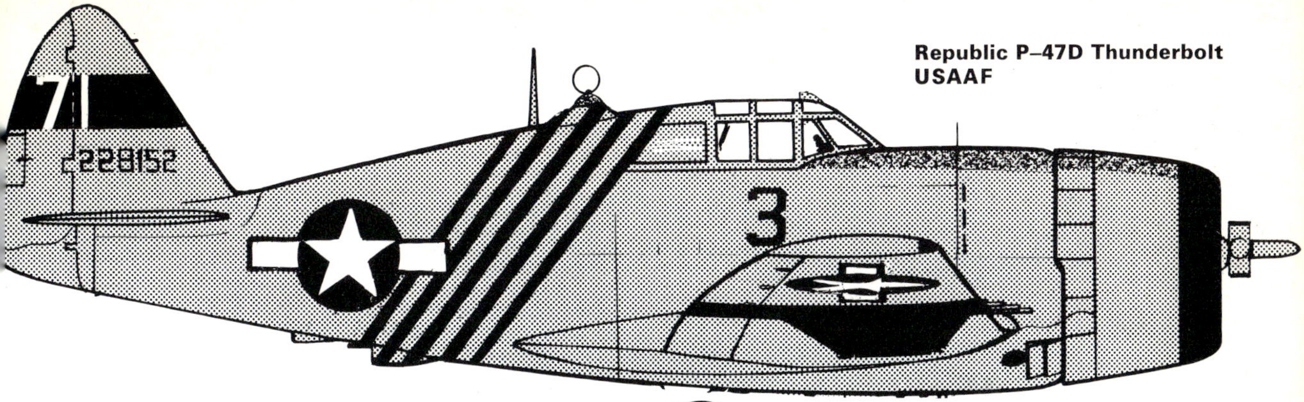

Starboard side details.

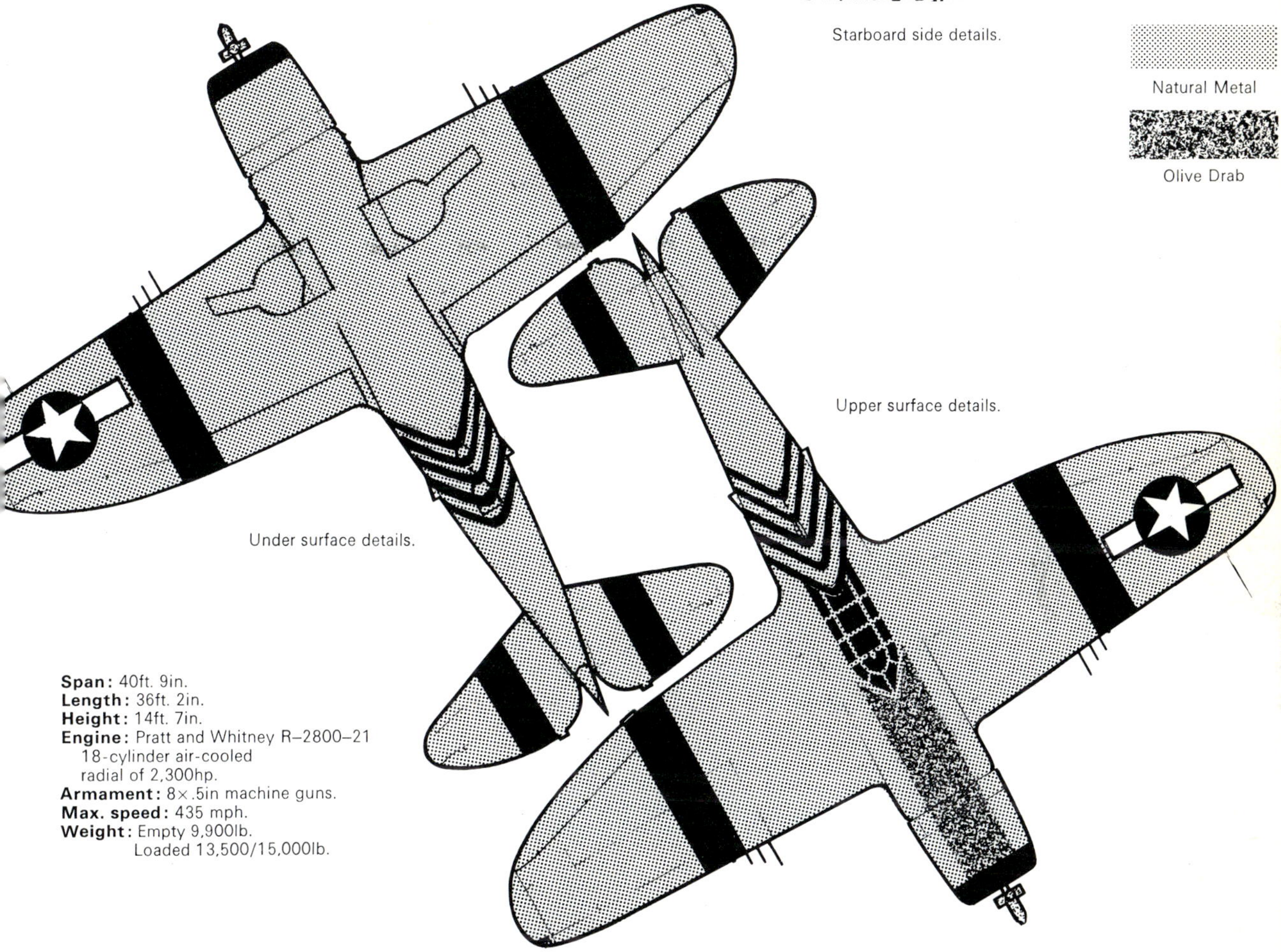

Upper surface details.

Under surface details.

Span: 40ft. 9in.
Length: 36ft. 2in.
Height: 14ft. 7in.
Engine: Pratt and Whitney R–2800–21 18-cylinder air-cooled radial of 2,300hp.
Armament: 8×.5in machine guns.
Max. speed: 435 mph.
Weight: Empty 9,900lb. Loaded 13,500/15,000lb.

P–47D Thunderbolt of the 1st Air Commando Group takes off on a long-range strafing mission from an airfield in India. Note the DF loop on the radio compass housing; a similarly marked P–47 carried the number 14 on the fin and rudder but no number on the fuselage. (USAF)

Republic P–47D Thunderbolt USAAF

Starboard side details.

Pale Grey

Olive Drab

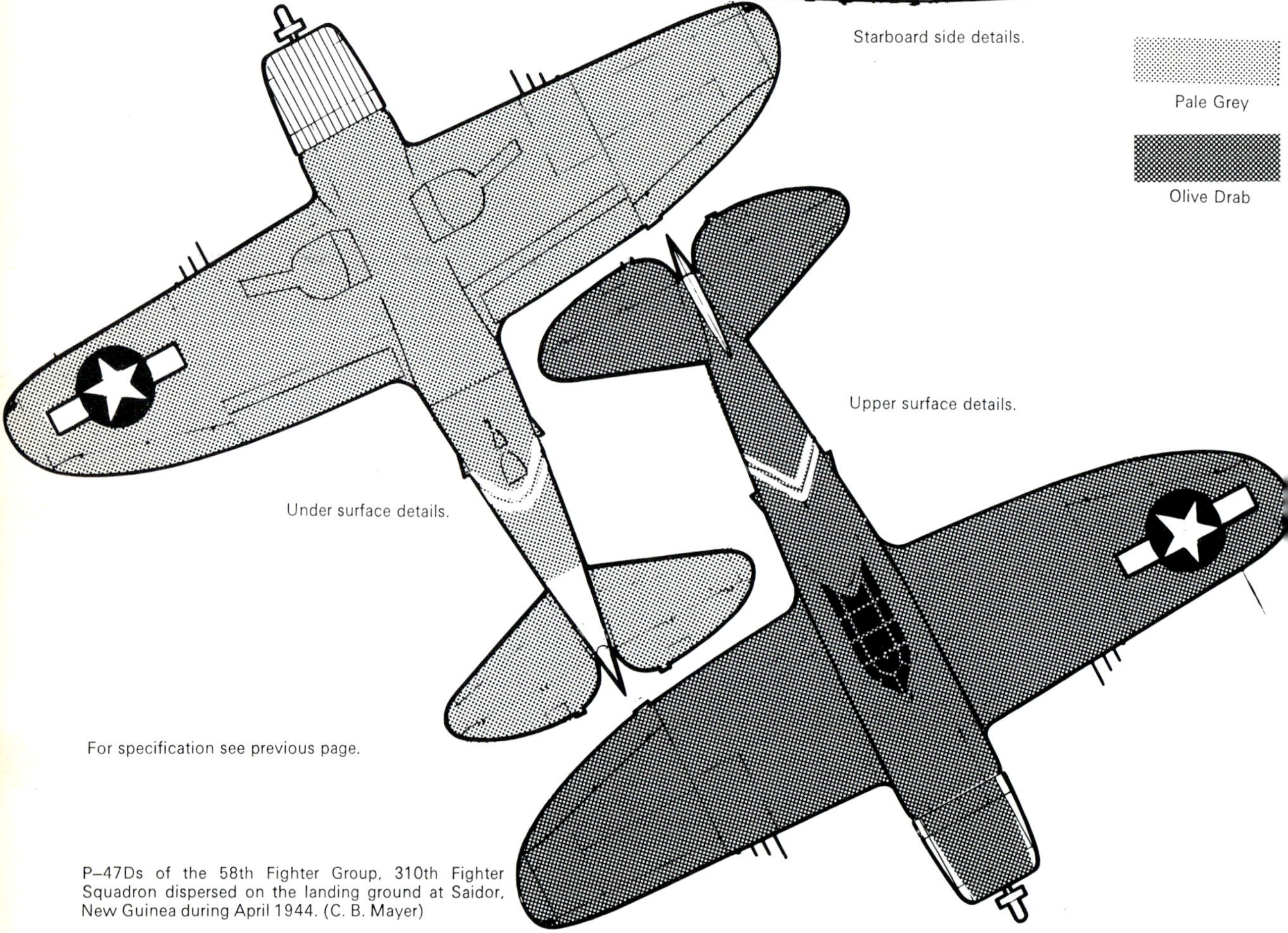

Upper surface details.

Under surface details.

For specification see previous page.

P–47Ds of the 58th Fighter Group, 310th Fighter Squadron dispersed on the landing ground at Saidor, New Guinea during April 1944. (C. B. Mayer)

Republic P–47D Thunderbolt
Chilean Air Force

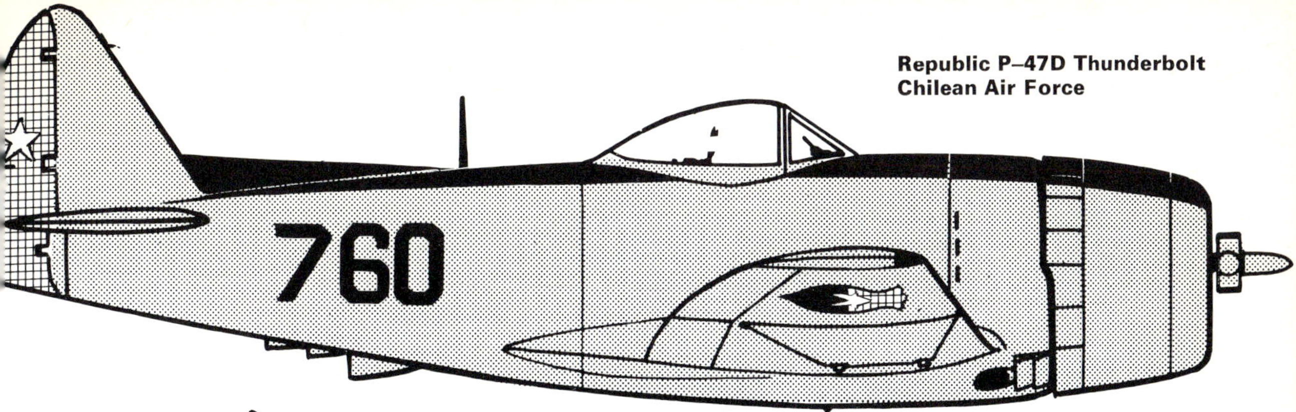

Starboard side details.

Natural Metal

Chilean Air Force insignia, white star on blue and red shield, red shown black.

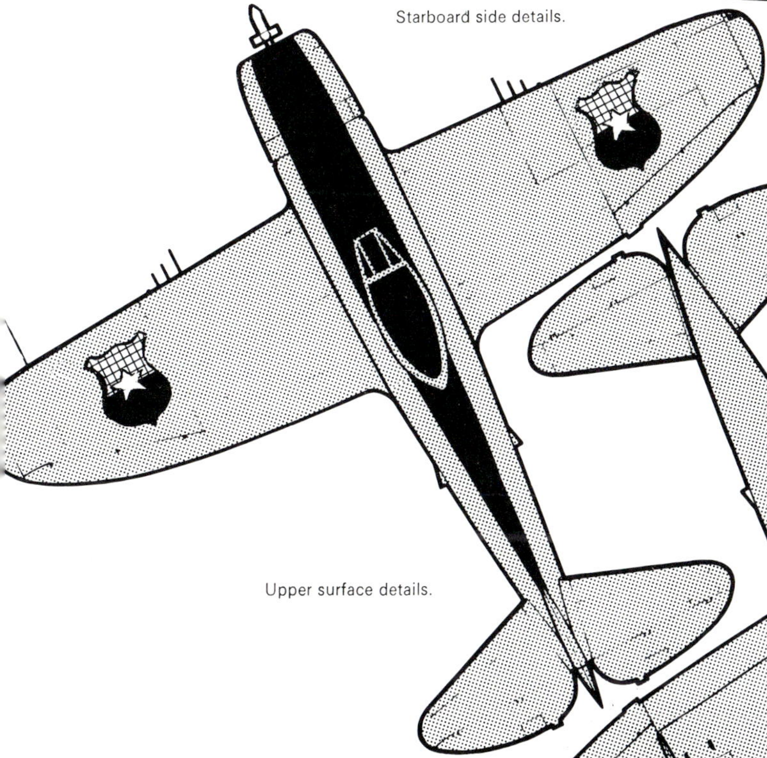

Upper surface details.

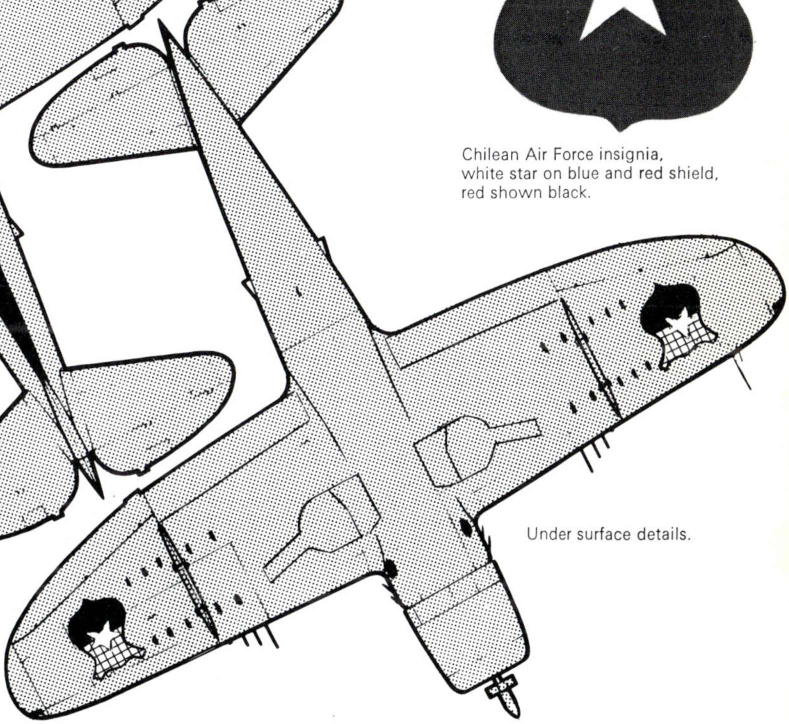

Under surface details.

The P–47D found its way into many air forces during the post-war years one of them being the Chilean of which an example is illustrated here. (USAF)

Vickers Supermarine Spitfire Mk.IX
Royal Canadian Air Force

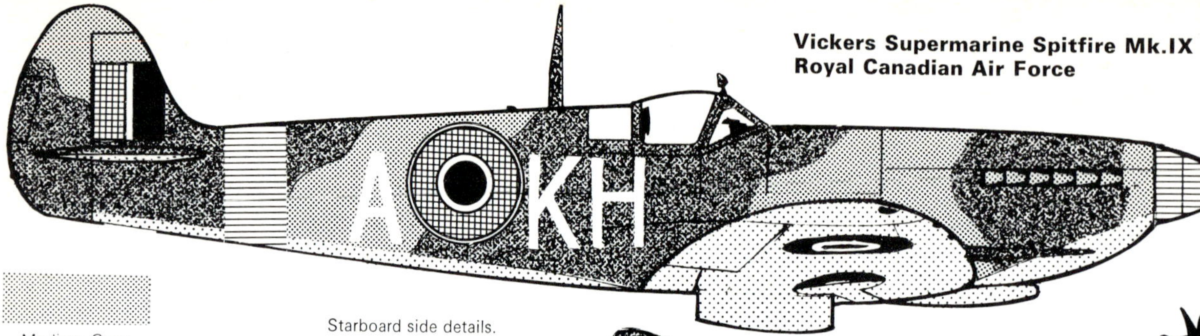

Starboard side details.

Medium Grey

Dark Green

Pale Grey

Wolf's head, port side only, black with red tongue and eye.

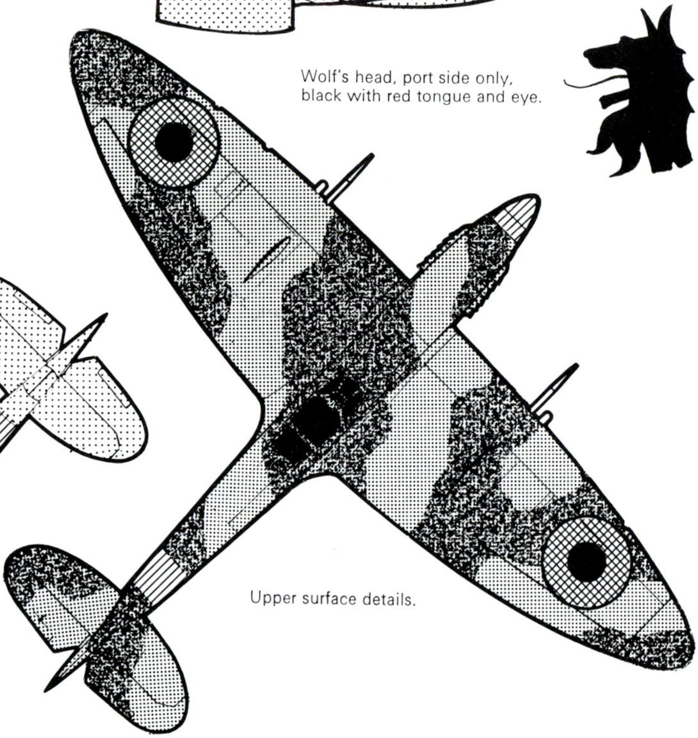

Upper surface details.

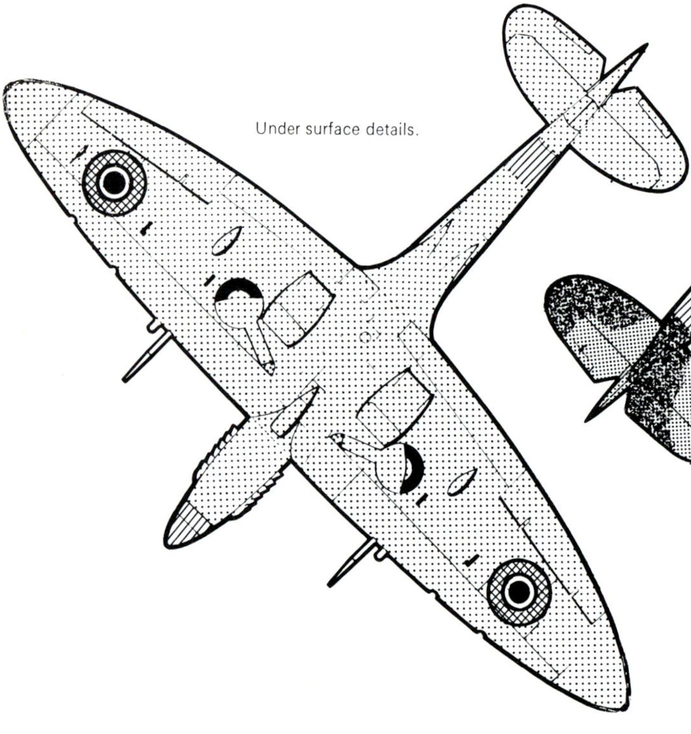

Under surface details.

Span: 32ft. 7in. **Length:** 31ft. 4in. **Height:** 12ft. 7in.
Engine: Rolls-Royce Merlin 66 12-cylinder liquid-cooled V of 1,720hp.
Armament: 2× 20mm cannon plus 2× .303in machine guns.
Max. speed: 404 mph.
Weight: Empty 5,800lb. Loaded 7,500lb.

Spitfire Mk.IX of No. 403 Squadron, 2nd TAF, RCAF, dispersed at Lympne, Kent during February of 1944.

Vickers Supermarine Spitfire Mk.IX French Air Force

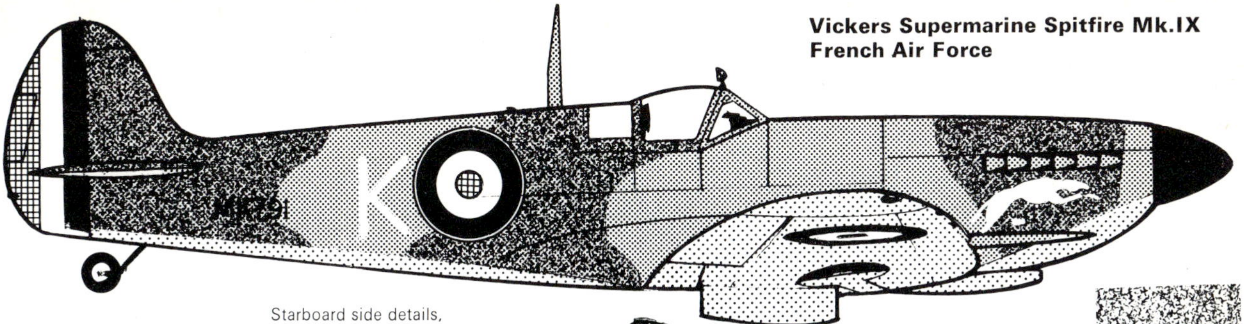

Starboard side details, note blue in roundel shown black.

Dark Green

Pale Grey

Medium Grey

Greyhound in white port and starboard.

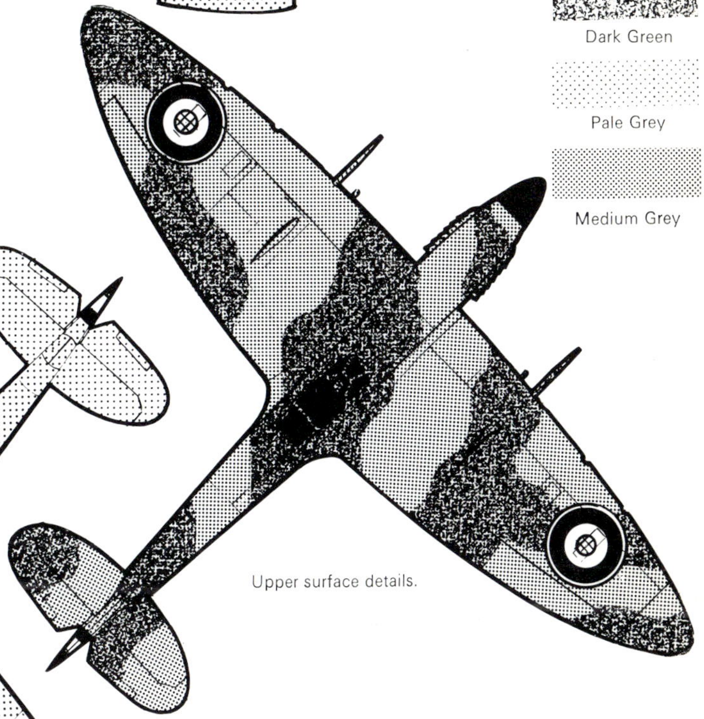

Upper surface details.

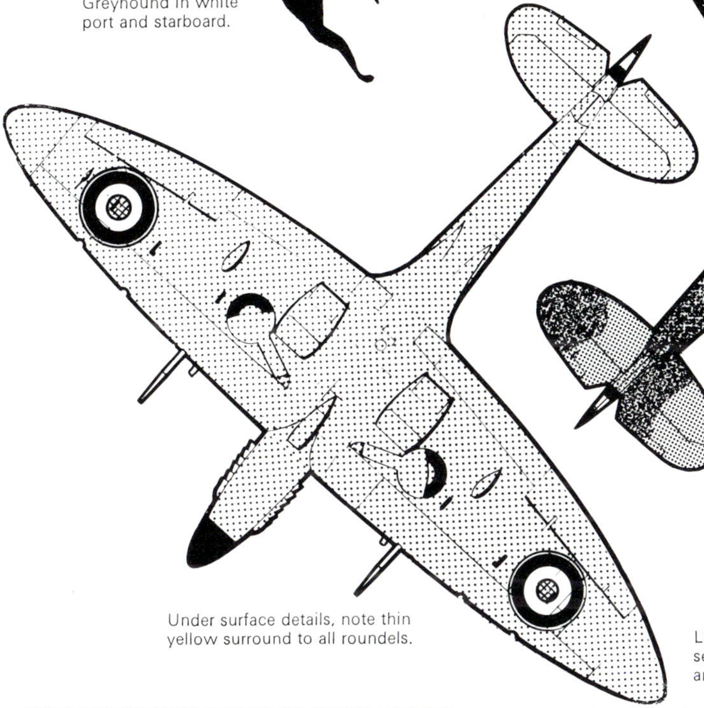

Under surface details, note thin yellow surround to all roundels.

Line-up of Spitfire Mk,IXs and Mk.XVIs on Hanoi airfield, the second Spitfire in the line-up is illustrated on the front cover and title page. (ECA via J. Cuny)

411210, the first XP–54 built which flew on 15 January 1943, in original configuration above and with extended fin below. (Peter M. Bowers)

Span: 53ft. 6in. **Length:** 54ft. 9in. **Height:** 14ft. 6½in.
Engine: Lycoming XH–2470–1 liquid-cooled of 2,300hp.
Armament: 2× 37mm cannon plus 2× .5in machine guns.
Max. speed: 405 mph estimated.
Weight: Empty 15,260lb. Loaded 18,235/19,375lb.

Vultee XP–54
USAAF

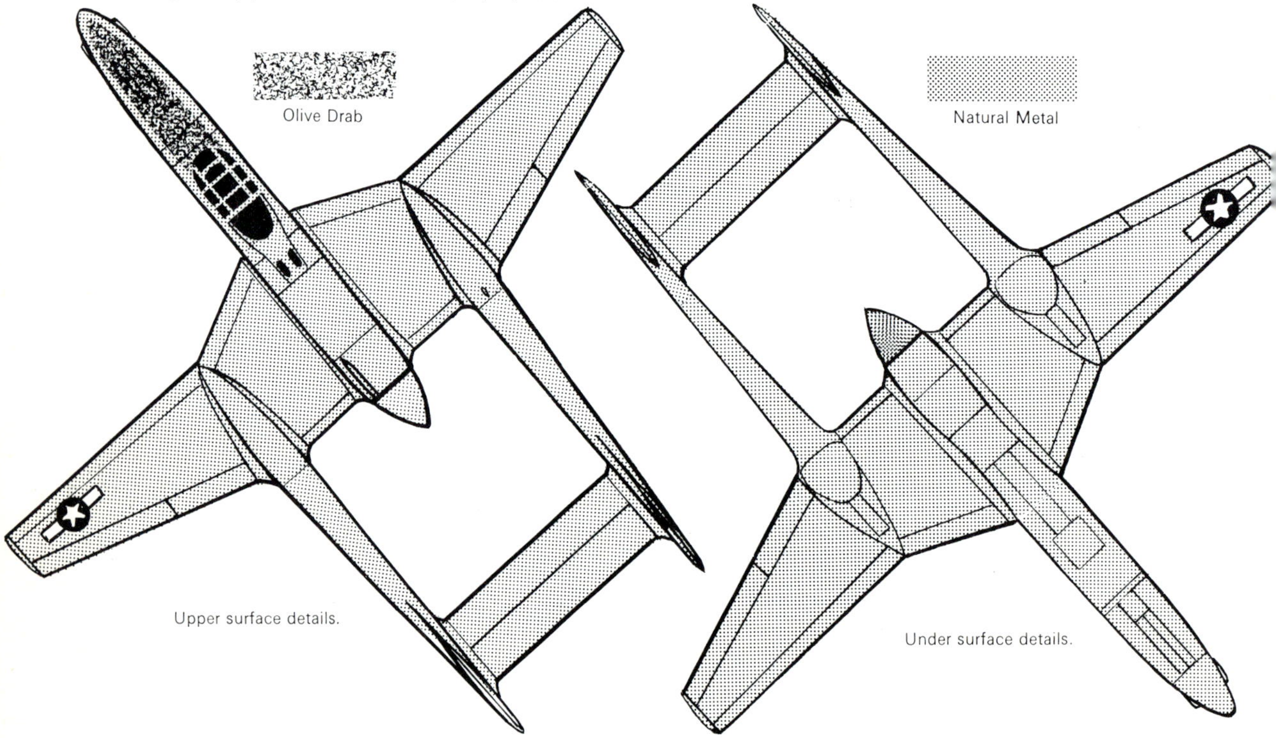

Upper surface details.

Under surface details.

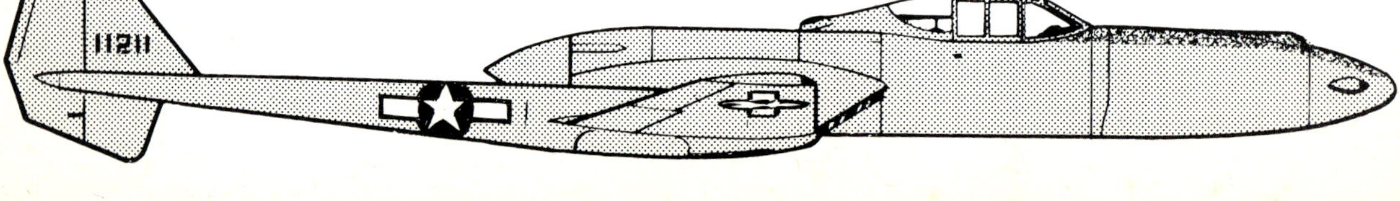

Starboard side details of the second prototype in natural metal finish.

Valtion Lentokonetehdas V.L. Myrsky II
Finnish Air Force

Starboard side details of MY–5.

Yellow

Olive Drab

Pale Blue

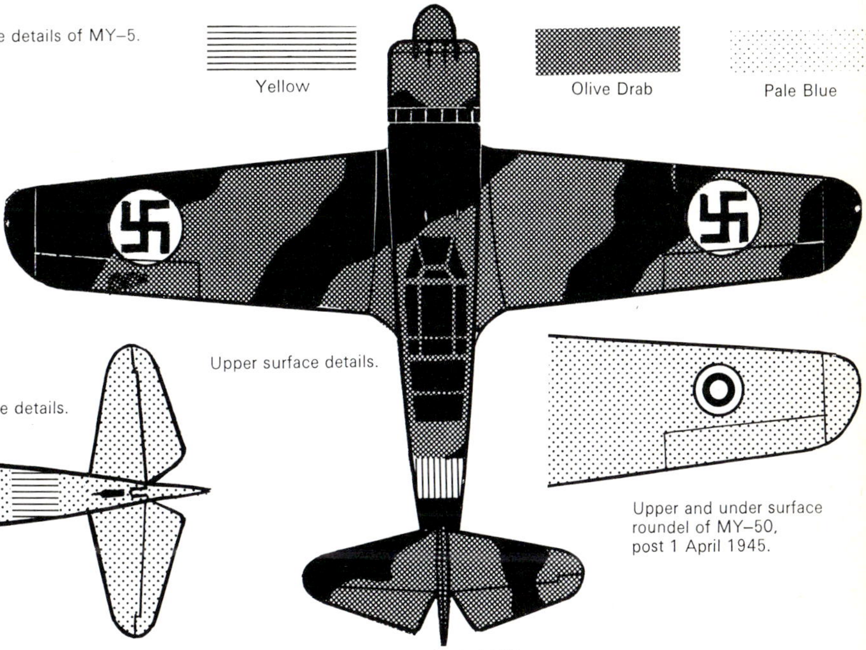

Upper surface details.

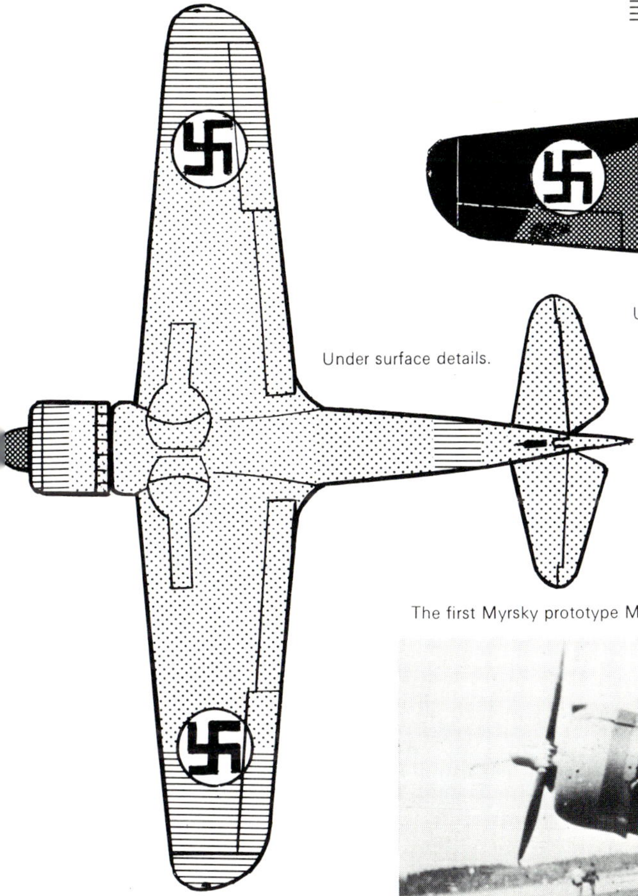

Under surface details.

Upper and under surface roundel of MY–50, post 1 April 1945.

The first Myrsky prototype MY–1 which crashed under test in 1942.

Span: SFA/Pratt and Whitney
Length: 27ft. 4½in.
Height: 9ft. 10in.
Engine: SFA/Pratt and Whitney Twin Wasp SC3–G 14-cylinder air-cooled radial of 1,065hp.
Armament: 4×12.7mm machine guns.
Max. speed: 330 mph.
Weight: Empty 5,140lb. Loaded 7,050lb.

MY–5 the third production aircraft into which were incorporated all the improvements found necessary during the testing of the two prototypes and first two production aircraft all of which crashed, the modifications resulted in MY–5 and all subsequent production aircraft being re-designated Myrsky II. Unpopular with pilots it saw very limited action against the retreating German armies. (Borge Heilm)

Kyushu J7W1 Shinden
Japanese Naval Air Service

Starboard side details.

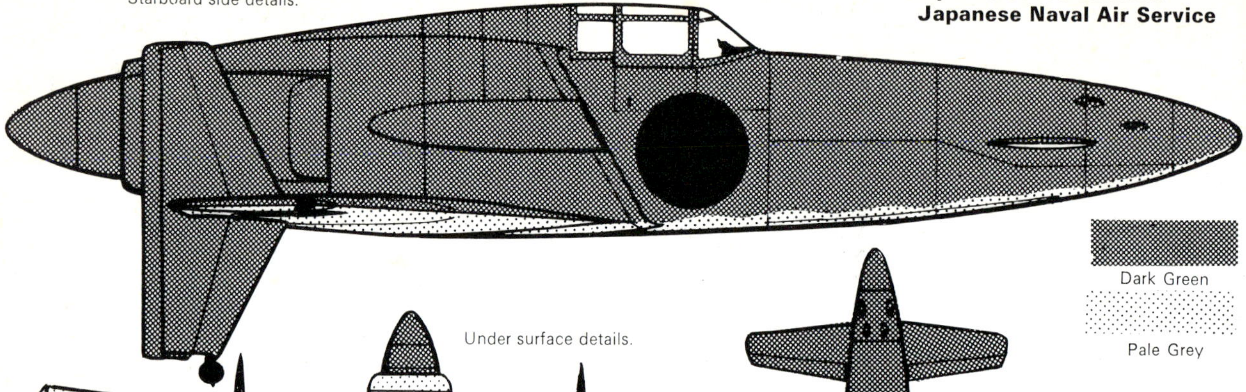

Dark Green

Pale Grey

Under surface details.

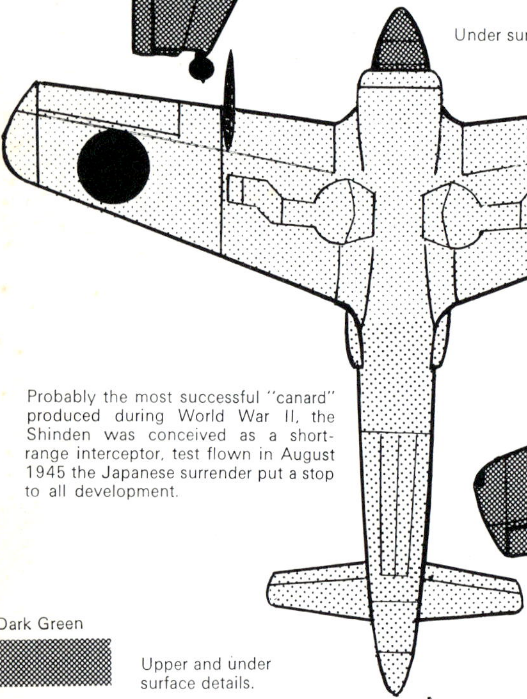

Upper surface details.

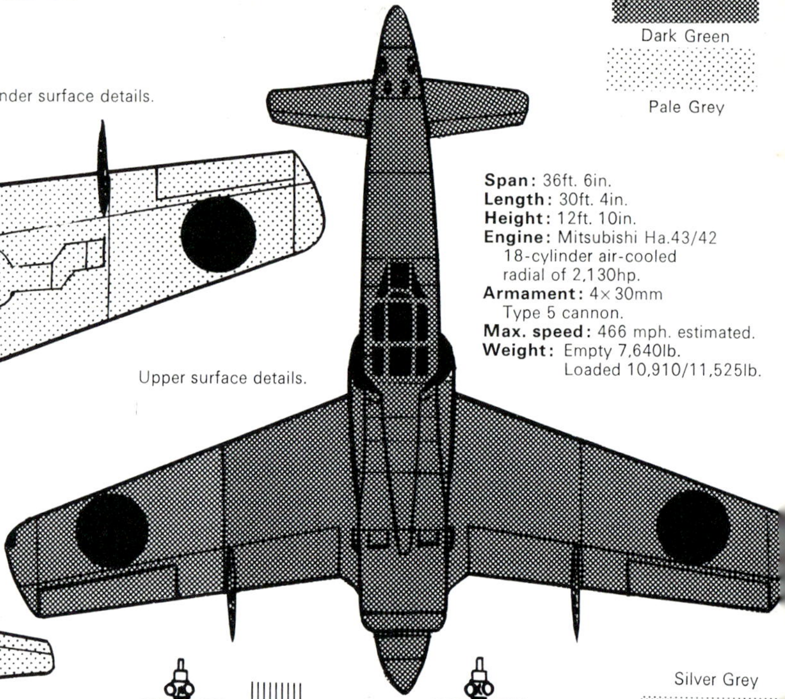

Span: 36ft. 6in.
Length: 30ft. 4in.
Height: 12ft. 10in.
Engine: Mitsubishi Ha.43/42 18-cylinder air-cooled radial of 2,130hp.
Armament: 4× 30mm Type 5 cannon.
Max. speed: 466 mph. estimated.
Weight: Empty 7,640lb. Loaded 10,910/11,525lb.

Probably the most successful "canard" produced during World War II, the Shinden was conceived as a short-range interceptor, test flown in August 1945 the Japanese surrender put a stop to all development.

Dark Green

Upper and under surface details.

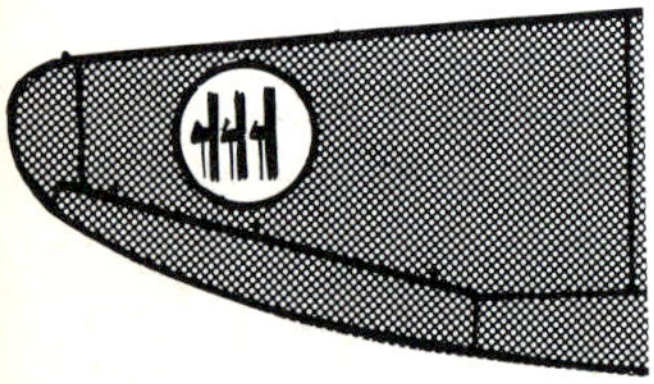

Yellow

Silver Grey

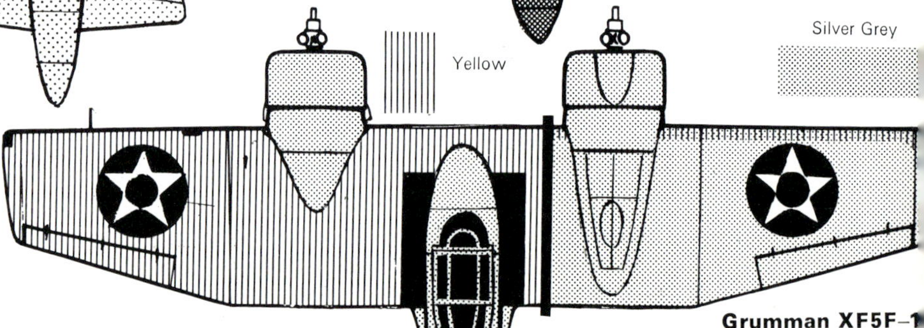

Grumman XF5F–1
US Navy

Upper and under surface details, yellow upper surface to mainplane, remainder of aircraft in silver grey. See No. S17 Vol. 1 for further details of the XF5F–1 and XP–50.

Starboard side details.
For performance figures see No. S17 Vol. 1.

REGGIANE Re.2001
REGIA AERONAUTICA

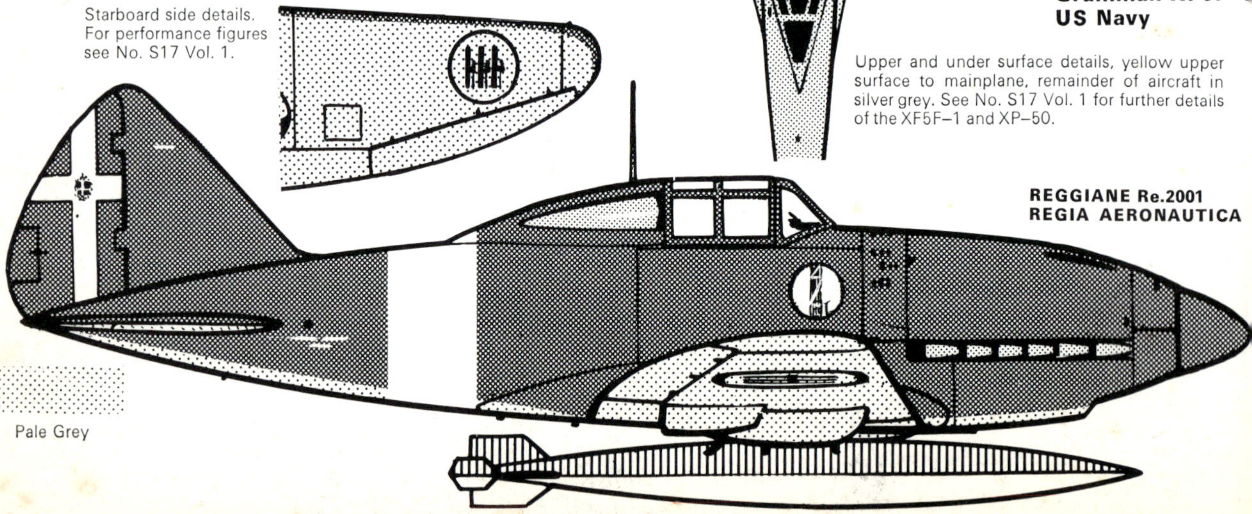

Pale Grey